The Church

The Church

Presbyterian Perspectives

Donald K. McKim

CASCADE *Books* • Eugene, Oregon

THE CHURCH
Presbyterian Perspectives

Copyright © 2017 Donald K. McKim. All rights reserved. Except for brief quotations in critical publications or reviews, no part of this book may be reproduced in any manner without prior written permission from the publisher. Write: Permissions, Wipf and Stock Publishers, 199 W. 8th Ave., Suite 3, Eugene, OR 97401.

Cascade Books
An Imprint of Wipf and Stock Publishers
199 W. 8th Ave., Suite 3
Eugene, OR 97401

www.wipfandstock.com

PAPERBACK ISBN: 978-1-5326-0053-1
HARDCOVER ISBN: 978-1-5326-0055-5
EBOOK ISBN: 978-1-5326-0054-8

Cataloguing-in-Publication data:

Names: McKim, Donald K., author.
Title: The church : Presbyterian perspectives / Donald K. McKim.
Description: Eugene, OR: Cascade Books, 2017 | Includes bibliographical references and index.
Identifiers: ISBN: 978-1-5326-0053-1 (paperback) | ISBN: 978-1-5326-0055-5 (hardcover) | ISBN: 978-1-5326-0054-8 (ebook).
Subjects: Church | Presbyterian Church—Doctrines.
Classification: BX9422.2 M36 2017 (print) | BX9422.2 (ebook)

Manufactured in the U.S.A.   02/13/17V

Excerpts from Calvin: *Institutes of the Christian Religion* (Library of Christian Classics) edited by John T. McNeill, trans. Ford Lewis Battles, ©1960. Used by kind permission of Westminster John Knox Press (www.wjkbooks.com).

With gratitude to my home congregation and the memory of
my pastor
Wampum Presbyterian Church
Wampum, Pennsylvania
Rev. John E. Karnes

And to the congregations I have served in ministry
Friendship Parish, Slippery Rock, Pennsylvania
West Liberty Presbyterian Church
Wolf Creek Presbyterian Church
Bethel Presbyterian Church
Trinity Presbyterian Church, Berwyn, Pennsylvania
Central Presbyterian Church, Downingtown, Pennsylvania

In memory of my parents, Keith and Mary McKim, who
nurtured me in the church
In memory of Alan P. F. Sell and Jack B. Rogers

Contents

Preface | ix

1. The Call to Follow Jesus in the Church | 1
2. The Church Reformed and Always Being Reformed according to the Word of God | 15
3. I Believe in the Holy Ghost | 31
4. I Believe in the Holy Catholic Church | 47
5. I Believe in the Communion of Saints | 64
6. Imagine the Church! | 79

Bibliography | 91

Preface

It is a pleasure to offer these theological reflections on the church. While the experience of church is common to many people, what is less common is theological reflection on the nature of the church. What is the church? What does it mean to be part of the people of God, the body of Christ, and the community of the Holy Spirit?

I hope these thoughts will bring insights to edify, comfort, and challenge those in churches. May we understand more fully and serve more faithfully as disciples of Jesus Christ. The church can be the focus of our discipleship in Christ where we learn of him. It can also be the locus, the place from which our ministries begin and are carried out in the world around us. To these purposes, this book is dedicated.

These reflections are written from my commitment as a Reformed theologian. I am a retired minister of the Presbyterian Church (U.S.A.) and have spent my life as a pastor, seminary professor and dean, and an editor for Westminster John Knox Press and Congregational Ministries Publishing of the Presbyterian Church (U.S.A.). In all these contexts and in the writing I've done, I have sought to be a church theologian. I have tried to probe our biblical and theological traditions to understand ways these can vitalize and energize our lives as disciples of Jesus Christ. All this is carried out in the context of the widest ecumenical commitment to seek the unity of Christ's church, as John Calvin (1509–1564) and other Reformed theologians have sought to do.

Preface

These chapters began as presentations to groups of clergy and laity through the years. "The Call to Follow Jesus in the Church" was shared at Synod of the Mid-Atlantic Presbyterian Men's Conference at Massanetta Springs, Virginia. It was energizing to be with church members who have an active interest in learning and serving the church, locally and globally.

The four chapters "The Church Reformed and Always Being Reformed according to the Word of God," "I Believe in the Holy Ghost," "I Believe in the Holy Catholic Church," and "I Believe in the Communion of Saints" were presented to the Omaha Presbyterian Seminary Foundation Summer Pastors' School at Hastings College in Hastings, Nebraska. This lively group of pastors was a most receptive audience who "live church" in their ministries every day. I am grateful for their faithful witness to Jesus Christ. I thank the Foundation's president, Dr. Gary Eller, for the invitation to my wife LindaJo and me to share lectures and this special week with dedicated servants of Christ. Gary kindly provided for us in every way and we are very grateful to him and for the full range of ministries he carries out in the church and beyond.

"Imagine the Church!" was presented at the First Presbyterian Church of Pittsford, New York. This lively congregation is well served by pastors Bruce Boak and Carrie Mitchell, whose friendship and hospitality to LindaJo and me is warmly remembered and deeply appreciated.

The chapters here, of course, do not provide a full discussion of the meaning of *church*. Far more needs to be said and reflected upon to develop a better sense of the wideness and fullness of the church of Jesus Christ. At best, these are first steps, some basics or essentials of ecclesiology, the study of the doctrine of the church. But my hope is these discussions will open new windows for further understanding and new doors for serving Jesus Christ as part of a community of faith.

I would like to thank Dr. Robin Parry of Wipf and Stock Publishers. Robin gave me good advice on this project and helped in getting the project established in the Cascade Books imprint of

Preface

this remarkable company. Copyeditor Jeremy Funk has been extremely helpful as well.

My family provides joys and delights and brings meaning to me, every day. My wife, LindaJo, is my dearest friend and companion as we share life and love together. I am overwhelmingly grateful to her. Our son, Stephen, and his wife, Caroline, with Maddie, Annie, and Jack bring freshness and vitality to us that makes us wonderfully happy. Our son, Karl, and his wife, Lauren, bring us gladness and blessings, always.

This book is dedicated to church congregations which have been meaningful to me through the years. The Wampum Presbyterian Church in Wampum, Pennsylvania, where our parents were active members, provided the growth and nurture that set me in the direction of Christian vocation. Rev. John E. Karnes had a major influence through my high school years, for which I am deeply grateful.

For eleven years I served as a student-supply and a stated-supply pastor of three congregations that had long histories as worshiping communities. The churches of Friendship Parish, Slippery Rock, Pennsylvania: West Liberty, Wolf Creek, and Bethel Presbyterian Churches were fully loving and kind to me through my years as a student and in PhD studies. They were a true "communion of saints."

During years in the Philadelphia area, I served as interim pastor for Trinity Presbyterian Church in Berwyn and the Central Presbyterian Church in Downingtown, Pennsylvania. These two fine congregations were "loyal companions" in ministry (Phil 4:3) and I am thankful when I remember them (Phil 1:3).

This book is also dedicated to the memory of my parents, Keith and Mary McKim. They provided love and nurture for my sister, Thelma, and me in our family home and local church. For them I am truly grateful.

The deaths of two dear friends and devoted servants of the church have left me saddened. Alan P. F. Sell, former theological secretary of the World Alliance of Reformed Churches, and Jack B. Rogers, seminary professor and moderator of the 2001 General

Preface

Assembly of the Presbyterian Church (U.S.A.), who was my teacher and coauthor died in recent months. Their lives and witness as church theologians are strong. They have certainly given me "an example to imitate" (2 Thess 3:9). I thank God for their lives.

My hope is that theological understandings of the church will enhance and deepen the faith of all readers. To God be "glory in the church and in Christ Jesus to all generations, forever and ever. Amen" (Eph 3:21).

Donald K. McKim
Germantown, Tennessee
January 2017

1 The Call to Follow Jesus in the Church

Some years ago, Dr. Ernest T. Campbell, who was the senior pastor of the Riverside Church in New York City and was a friend, preached a sermon that has meant much to me. In it, Dr. Campbell focused on the call of the disciples and the simple words of Jesus: "Follow me."[1] Though it was preached over forty years ago, Campbell's points continue to speak to us with passion and power. In considering "The Call to Follow Christ in the Church," I would like to enlarge on Ernest Campbell's insights.

Every journey has its starting point. The trip to the store, the visit to friends, the vacation across the country; all have to begin somewhere. So too with the journey of faith. We have all started somewhere, at some time. We have heard the words of Jesus: "Follow me" (Mark 1:17). And we have responded to that call. For some the call to follow came at a definite time and place. It is possible to know the exact instant at which the call was heard and our response was made. Perhaps this experience was very dramatic—as for the apostle Paul, who was struck blind on the road to Damascus (Acts 9:1–9). Or John Wesley, who said he felt his heart "strangely warmed" when he heard the gospel. Or, John Calvin, who spoke of his "sudden conversion." The call to follow Jesus Christ has broken into our lives and changed them very powerfully.

---

1. Campbell, "Follow Me."

Or, perhaps the call to follow came at a definite time, but very quietly. The voice of Jesus was unmistakable. And you said yes to that voice in the stillness and the quietness of your own heart.

But for many on the journey of faith, the beginnings have long since been forgotten. All of life, even from earliest days, has been lived with the consciousness that Jesus Christ is continually calling you. There was no one certain day or time when you first remember hearing the voice. It seems always to have been there saying, "Follow me." And you have been following all your days. The start has been made. But when it was made or even why it was made is a mystery.

What does it mean to "follow" Jesus Christ today? We may wonder if this is any more than a slogan, a catchphrase from anyone who for some reason wishes to identify herself or himself with the man Jesus. How does the call to follow Jesus come today? There are many voices we hear all around us, crying out for any number of causes and programs. Promotions are made on behalf of everyone—from politicians to rock stars to religious leaders. In the midst of so many voices, can the voice of Jesus be heard? What does it sound like? What does Jesus ask of us in terms of lifestyle if we respond to the call to follow?

Since we are used to a complex world, we are startled by the simple responses of those first disciples. The Gospels tell us that to Matthew, a tax collector, a man engaged in a profession hated by his fellow citizens, Jesus said, "Follow me. And he got up and followed him" (Mark 2:14). Peter and Andrew were brothers in the fishing business. Jesus said to them: "Follow me and I will make you fish for people. And immediately they left their nets and followed him" (Mark 1:17–18). Luke says they "left everything and followed him" (Luke 5:11). Similarly, Jesus called James and John—the sons of Zebedee. The record is that "immediately he called them; and they left their father Zebedee in the boat with the hired men, and followed him" (Mark 1:19–20).

Such instant and willing responses leave us shaking our heads! How could they do it? Did they know what they were getting into? Must the call to follow come to us with such a force and demand from us such a dramatic reaction? A few years ago, Professor Adam Copeland wrote in the *Christian Century*: "When Jesus called to Peter and Andrew on the beach, he did not say, 'Here are my long-term objectives. Talk my proposal through with your stakeholders at your annual meeting and let me know if your analysis suggests the mission is scalable.'"[2] The disciples of Jesus didn't have to "think it through," consider the alternatives, or develop complicated plans. It's like Casey Stengel said about baseball: "There's three things that can happen in baseball. Either you win or you lose or it rains." It's that simple. We can either follow Jesus or not follow Jesus. If we do nothing at all and just drift along aimlessly in life, we've chosen not to follow. But the first disciples made the positive decision. They "immediately" left their nets and followed him.

Throughout the Scriptures, Jesus seeks this type of immediate, committed response from all he calls to follow him. His words are strikingly blunt. Jesus told his disciples that "if any want to become my followers, let them deny themselves and take up their cross and follow me" (Matt 16:24); and "whoever does not take up the cross and follow me is not worthy of me" (Matt 10:38). He said, "Sell all that you own and distribute the money to the poor . . . then come, follow me" (Luke 18:22). His thrust is unmistakable: To respond to the call to follow is to make a commitment of one's self to the person of Jesus. Those unwilling to commit themselves so radically need not apply to be a follower. As Jesus put it with characteristic candor, "Follow me, and let the dead bury their own dead" (Matt 8:22; cf. Luke 9:61–62). This radical commitment is the same God demanded in the Old Testament. In the showdown with the prophets of Baal, Elijah on Mount Carmel told the people: "If the Lord is God, follow [the Lord]" (1 Kgs 18:21). Followers of Jesus left families and professions behind in the interest of a new loyalty, a greater love. As theologian Karl Barth put it: "The call issued by Jesus is a call to discipleship."[3]

---

2. Copeland, "Why Lead?," 12.
3. Barth, *Church Dogmatics*, IV/2, 533.

What does it mean to "follow Jesus" today? How do we understand the call to follow in our own contexts, in the midst of our busy, pressure-packed lives?

Here are three theological perspectives on discipleship as we have them in the New Testament. These are foundations for all we do as followers of Jesus, as disciples of our Lord and Master.

We Are Joined with Jesus

The first dimension of discipleship is that in discipleship, we are joined with Jesus. Those whom Jesus called followed him; and they were joined with Jesus in the totality of their lives. Jesus called them, "elected" them, "ordained" them to be his disciples. They responded; and now their lives are forever changed. Their worlds are turned upside down because they now have a new loyalty, a greater love. They are attached or joined with Jesus.

The New Testament calls this joining, "faith." Faith is the gift of God. It is a gift given to us so we recognize who Jesus is. The Spirit of God works faith in our hearts, just as faith became the way of life for those first disciples. In faith, we are bound to the One who calls us—Jesus Christ. In following Jesus, we are not called to adopt a program, or an ideal, or a law—all things that we might attempt to fulfill. In following Jesus, we are called to faith in the person of Jesus Christ himself. We believe Jesus is the eternal Son of God, the Savior of the world, the One who has reconciled the world to God in his life, death, and resurrection. Jesus Christ brings the fullness of salvation. Faith is our way of being joined with Jesus. In faith we confess who Jesus is; we believe in him. We trust him. We give our whole selves to him, to be his disciples and followers. As theologian Karl Barth said, "In practice the command to follow Jesus is identical with the command to believe in Him." To paraphrase Barth further, following Jesus means we put our trust in God as the God who is faithful to us the unfaithful; who in spite of our own forgetfulness has not forgotten us; who without any cooperation or merit on our part wills that we should live and not die. In the call of Jesus we are met by the fulfilled promise of God as valid for us.[4]

So discipleship is very personal. It is response to the call of God in Jesus Christ (which we Presbyterians call election) to join us with Jesus by faith. Theologian Dietrich Bonhoeffer said, "The call to discipleship here has no other content than Jesus Christ himself, being bound to him, community with him."[5] In discipleship, we are joined with Jesus.

We Are Obedient to Jesus

The second dimension is that in discipleship, we are obedient to Jesus. Bonhoeffer pointed out that in the calling of the disciples, "the disciple's answer [to Jesus's call] is not a spoken confession of faith in Jesus. Instead, it is the obedient deed."[6] Jesus called, and expected a response of obedience. Bonhoeffer noted that "the forces that wanted to get between the word of Jesus and obedience were just as great back then as they are today. Reason objected; Conscience, responsibility, [and] piety" objected.[7] There were many, many reasons why "it wouldn't be prudent" for those earliest followers to leave everything and follow Jesus. But this is precisely what they did. Again, as Bonhoeffer wrote: "The road to faith passes through obedience to Christ's call."[8]

Our believing and entrusting ourselves to the person of Jesus means he is our Lord and Master, it means we bring all things in our lives under the Lordship and control of Jesus Christ as his obedient followers. As Barth put it: "What Jesus demands is trust in Himself and therefore, in the concrete form which this involves, trust in God. He demands faith in the form of obedience, obedience to Himself. This is the commitment to Him which constitutes

---

4. Ibid., 536.
5. Bonhoeffer, *Discipleship*, 74.
6. Ibid., 57.
7. Ibid., 77.
8. Ibid., 63.

the content of the call to discipleship."⁹ "Simple obedience" (Bonhoeffer) is what God requires.

Later, in the New Testament, Paul speaks about "the obedience of faith" when he writes of "Jesus Christ our Lord, through whom we have received grace and apostleship to bring about the obedience of faith" (Rom 1:5; cf. 16:26). The goal, for Paul, is a total obedience. It is obedience to Jesus Christ in all we are and all we do. Obedience is to be comprehensive, throughout our lives. The goal says Paul is that "we take every thought captive to obey Christ" (2 Cor 10:5). Imagine that! Even every *thought* is to be captive to obey Christ. And if every thought is to obey Christ, then what of every action and activity? As the hymn puts us, God's love in Christ, "demands my soul, my life, my all."¹⁰ In discipleship, we are obedient to Jesus.

We Yield to Jesus

Then, third in discipleship, we yield to Jesus. Our obedience is in hearing Jesus's word, believing it, and acting on it. Our yielding to Jesus is our denial of our selves and our own agendas for life so that we will "leave our self behind" to follow Jesus. We yield to him. For Barth, "to follow Jesus means to go beyond oneself in a specific action and attitude, and therefore to turn one's back upon oneself, to leave oneself behind."¹¹ As Jesus said, "If any want to become my followers, let them deny themselves and take up their cross and follow me" (Mark 8:34). Some have said that this is the central ethical message of Jesus. In faith and obedience, we put Jesus at the center of our lives, seeking his way and his will, and not our own.

When we have times of conflict, times when there is what Christ wants us to do; and what we want to do—which do we choose? The temptation to "do it my way," as the old Frank Sinatra song put it, is strong. We'd like to satisfy: "Me, myself, and I." This is

---

9. Barth, *Church Dogmatics*, IV/2, 537.

10. Isaac Watts, "When I Survey the Wondrous Cross," in L. H. McKim, ed., *The Presbyterian Hymnal*, #101.

11. Barth, *Church Dogmatics*, IV/2, 538.

our natural pull, our natural desire. To fulfill our self-desire—that is our natural urge. But as followers of Christ, we yield to Jesus. We put the will and purposes of Jesus at the center, as the primary motivation and direction for our lives—in all things. We say, "Not mine, but thine," "not me, but thee." Christ is at the center; we yield ourselves to him. John Calvin wrote that when the denial of self has taken possession of our hearts, "it leaves no place at all first either to pride, or arrogance, or ostentation; then either to avarice, or desire, or . . . to other evils that our self-love spawns."[12] In self-denial, said Calvin, we have "cut off the root of all evils so as to seek no longer the things that are [our] own."[13] As Jesus himself prayed in the garden of Gethsemane: "Not my will but yours be done" (Luke 22:42). This is our prayer as followers of Jesus. In discipleship, we yield to Jesus.

So this is the nature of our discipleship. In discipleship, we are joined with Jesus; we are obedient to Jesus; and we yield to Jesus. Think of the first letters of these three points. They are *j* for *joined*, *o* for *obedient*, and *y* for *yield*: J-O-Y. That spells joy! Ultimately this is what following Jesus brings us: joy. Through all the ups and downs of the Christian life; all the zigs and zags of following all—through them all, there is joy in the journey. Karl Barth said, "The command of Jesus is naturally to be heard and accepted and followed with joy. It is the commanding grace of God, and therefore the salvation of the whole world and of [humanity], entering [our] life as a free offer. How can [we] resist it?"[14] Yes, how can we resist the call of Jesus: "Follow me"? Our joy is in the journey of discipleship, all along our way; and in the ending of our following, as well—eternal life. Now, step by step, we rejoice in the joy of following Jesus: joined, obedient, and yielding to Jesus. Now we live, as Jesus promised: "I am the light of the world. Whoever *follows* me will never walk in darkness but will have the light of life" (John 8:12). We have the light—and the joy—of life, in following Jesus Christ.

12. Calvin, *Institutes* 3.7.2.
13. Ibid., 3.15.8.
14. Barth, *Church Dogmatics*, IV/2, 541.

So what does it mean for us to follow Jesus in this way? What does our discipleship look like? Here Dr. Campbell's points are helpful.

First, "Follow me" connects us with someone who is going somewhere.

As followers of Jesus we are a people on the move, a people with a destination. We do not just move for the sake of moving. Nor do we wander aimlessly, without purpose. We follow Jesus and he was supremely a person with a purpose. We all crave leadership. In government or our community, or in our church we look to those who can lead. We want someone with a clear vision of where we should be headed. This type of leadership is a rare quality. Since it is rare, we are tempted to back off, just to coast and let things happen—even to hibernate.

There's a certain therapy of hibernation. It's easy to slip into and like the law of inertia, it puts us at rest and keeps us there. I remember hearing Dr. David Stitt, president of Austin Seminary, once tell of a dog whining in a general store in West Texas. When a customer asked why the dog was whining, the owner said, "Because he's lying on a burr." The customer said, "Then why doesn't he move?" And the owner replied, "Because it's easier to whine than it is to move!" And so it is. It is easier to whine, to stay where we are, than to move out and move on. With all the voices today, all clamoring for attention, we wonder whom we should trust to lead. Whom shall we follow? We don't want to be like that bumper sticker that says: "Don't follow me. I'm lost!"

But Jesus is going somewhere. And the good news of the gospel is that Jesus calls us to follow. Jesus has a plan. Jesus has a purpose to achieve in human history and beyond. The good news is that Jesus cuts us in on the action. Jesus invites us to follow and be part of his work in history. Now that's a staggering thought! Think of it: Jesus invites you and me—the "likes of us"—to be his disciples and follow him! Amazing!

The word *follow* has as its root word in the Greek word for "road." To follow someone is to share the same road. To be with Jesus is to be on the move. The Christian life is an active life. We share the same road with Jesus; we follow where he leads. We attach ourselves to the purposes and plan of God in Jesus Christ. We share in the eternal destination toward which Jesus Christ is moving. So the Christian's prayer is not a *"longer stay* with God" but a *"closer walk* with God."[15]

This is the nature of Christian discipleship as following Jesus. We can not and do not need to know in advance where we are going, or how we will get there in following Jesus. But we entrust ourselves to Jesus Christ as the one who leads and guides us. Those first disciples, as Bonhoeffer put it, were "entrusting themselves to the word of Jesus Christ, believing it to be a stronger foundation than all the securities of the world."[16] No other word can provide what we need—no matter what it is. The word of Jesus to "Follow me"—that is enough. As Bonhoeffer also said, "Only Jesus Christ, who bids us follow him, knows where the path will lead. But we know that it will be a path full of mercy beyond measure. Discipleship is joy."[17]

Activity, movement, and growth occur in our Christian lives. Without these, we are not truly followers. We move forward with Jesus as we follow where he leads us. We are connected with someone who is going somewhere.

Second, to follow Jesus makes us more interested in the future than the past.

We need direction if we are to go somewhere. We also need a sense of loyalty to the future. Without this, we are stuck where we are, going around in circles. Jesus was tremendously oriented to the future. For Jesus it was not where you have been that matters; but

---

15. Campbell, "Follow Me," 2.
16. Bonhoeffer, *Discipleship*, 77.
17. Ibid., 40.

where you are going. For Jesus, it was not where you have fallen that matters, but will you get up? For Jesus, it was not whom you've hurt along the way, but will you help others in the future that counts?

Campbell points out that this is how Jesus moved through life. Many people have a problem with the past. They are paralyzed by the past, unable to move beyond it. Perhaps it was a bad childhood or a broken relationship or a bad experience with a church. But it leaves them unable to cope, unable to care, unable to move on in the journey of faith. Counselors can help. The problems of the past can be identified. But the real question is, can you go on to the next step? Can you cast out the past in the interests of moving toward the future to which Jesus Christ calls you?

Jesus didn't spend much time letting people unburden their pasts to him. When the woman taken in adultery was presented, Jesus didn't probe the circumstances. He didn't try to sort out all the details. Instead, he said, simply, "Go your way, and from now on do not sin again" (John 8:11). When Nicodemus came to Jesus at night, with all his hang-ups about legalism, Jesus didn't ask him how he got this way: "Was it overbearing parents that made you like this, Nick?" No. Instead, Jesus said, simply, "You must be born from above" (John 3:7). And the prodigal son (where we see the paradigm or mode of how God deals with failures)—in that story, the younger son never got to recited his memorized speech to his father. Instead, when the son cam dragging home, the father smothered him with love, and restored him to the full status as a child. To be penitent with God is to be forgiven, to be forgiven is to rise up and follow in discipleship.[18]

Of course we will not be perfect. One of the historic differences between Presbyterians in the Reformed theological tradition and the Methodists in the tradition of John Wesley is that the Wesleyans have believed that some form of perfection is possible for Christians in this life. But we Presbyterians don't believe we can be perfect, this side of heaven. We will fall again, and we will fail again and again. That's why when Christians gather to worship,

18. See Campbell, "Follow Me," 2–3.

in our tradition, the worship service features a prayer of confession. Christians who are followers of Jesus still sin. As the saying goes, Christians are not perfect, just forgiven. Our failures will still be real. We will always need forgiveness, over and over. But to move on as followers of Jesus, we will set out on that road with Jesus knowing that all along we are being led by his light and his love. I have always loved the quote from T. W. Manson, the British New Testament scholar who wrote: "The living Christ still has two hands, one to point the way, and the other held out to help us along. So the Christian ideal lies before us, not as a remote and austere mountain peak, an ethical Everest which we must scale by our own skill and endurance; but as a road on which we may walk with Christ as guide and friend. And we are assured, as we set out on the journey, that he is with us always, 'even unto the end of the world' (Matt 28:20)."[19]

We celebrate the future. We are confident that our past does not hold us captive; that we can follow Jesus Christ into the future he calls us toward—as a church, and as disciples of Jesus Christ, knowing that Christ's presence and power will sustain us all the way! To follow Jesus makes us more interested in the future than in the past.

Third, to follow Jesus means Jesus has given us the norm, the standard, by which to test our living.

Notice that in the Gospel stories of the call of the disciples, Jesus invites his followers to "follow" him. They are to follow, not to imitate him. In 1896, Charles Sheldon published a famous book called *In His Steps* that sold twenty-five million copies. It was the story of a town where for one year, every resident would ask a question before making any decision or taking any action. The question was, "What would Jesus do?" In recent years, there have been bracelets worn by a lot of people with the initialism WWJD on them. This stands for "What Would Jesus Do?" It is a good question. We

---

19. Manson, *Ethics and the Gospel*, 68.

need reminders to look to Jesus before we do something. Give us more folks in the church who ask this question! Yet in one sense, this is not the best question. Instead of what would Jesus do? we really should ask, what would Jesus have *me* do? The reason this question is better is that there is a distance between the Master and the servant, between Jesus and us. This distance will always be there, given who Jesus is and who we are. We will never live up to the life Jesus lived. We are his disciples, which literally means his "learners"—those who learn from their Master. We "follow" Jesus where we are in the contexts of the lives we live in the twenty-first century. No matter where we live, no matter who we are, we *can* follow Jesus—anytime, anywhere.

If you want a snapshot, an instant, capsulized picture of the whole of our Christian lives, this one phrase can be it: "To follow Jesus." This should constantly be our primary thought and direction. All church committees need to remember it. In this option or that, will we be moving our church in the direction Jesus is going? Will this action be consistent with what we know of the life of Jesus and what Jesus calls his followers to be and do? We ask it of ourselves as well. Others may not always agree with us, just as we will not always agree with other followers along the way. But the one thing we cannot question is our basic goal. As Christians, we are committed to following Jesus in all areas of life. There is no segment of life where Jesus is not our Master and our Lord. When we look to our actions, they must be judged in light of Jesus himself.

In his sermon, Dr. Campbell told the story of how a few days after John F. Kennedy was assassinated, a member of the church Dr. Campbell was serving in Ann Arbor, Michigan, called and suggested that the one thing the church might do partially to redeem the tragedy would be to provide Marina Oswald, wife of the accused assassin, an opportunity to improve her English. Mrs. Oswald had expressed the desire to stay in the United States and learn the language better. So representatives of the church got in touch with Marina Oswald. With the cooperation of the FBI and others, Mrs. Oswald came to Ann Arbor. She slipped quietly into town by train while a battery of reporters waited for her at the airport. She lived with a modest family that took seriously its devotion to God and its love for people. When the pressure mounted to make an announcement of what was done, the mail began to come in. There were some who were quick and hot to say that what the church did was unpatriotic. Others said the action was unwise, others that it was unfair. One woman wrote that she had belonged to a church for forty years and that what it had done for her in all that time she could write on the back of a postage stamp! Others were prompted to say that what was done was grossly un-American. But Dr. Campbell answered each letter personally, feeling it was part of his ministry to do so. And he said in effect to all who criticized: "The one thing you haven't shown us is that what we have done is unlike Christ."[20]

This is the challenge for the church, our congregational ministries, and our own discipleship as followers of Jesus. It doesn't ultimately matter if an action is popular or unpopular, practical, or realistic, whether it gains praise from people or whether it draws their criticism. What matters most, and always, is whether what we are and what we do can be understood as following Jesus Christ. It is Jesus himself who is the norm for our conduct.

This is, if you will, a christological ethic. We look to Jesus who is, as the book of Hebrews says, "the pioneer and perfecter of our faith" (Heb 12:2). Jesus Christ is the One who orients our lives and provides the star by which we steer our desires and actions. Another way to put it is this: that Jesus did not come to help us to *reach our goals*. Jesus came to help us *set our goals*. It is not what we want; it is what Jesus wants of us. It is not what we do for ourselves that counts; it's what we do for Jesus. It is not where we want to go; it is where Jesus wants us to go. We follow him.

It isn't always easy. In fact, we should expect that it will *not* be easy to follow Jesus. The experiences of Jesus's first disciples; and the millions of Christian believers who have lived through the centuries are witnesses to what Dietrich Bonhoeffer called "the cost of discipleship." When we are joined to Jesus in faith, seek to be obedient to Jesus, and yield to Jesus, we will face hostility in

---

20. Campbell, "Follow Me," 4–5.

various forms, as the book of Hebrews says. But through it all, we look to Jesus. We focus on the "pioneer and perfecter of our faith, who for the sake of the joy that was set before him endured the cross" (Heb 12:2). We can endure whatever sufferings we encounter because we are focused on Jesus Christ. Jesus said he would be "with [us] always, to the end of the age" as he promised his disciples (Matt 28:20). We share the witness and message of Jesus Christ, proclaiming salvation, peace, justice, and liberation to the world—because we have responded in faith to the call to follow Jesus. Jesus Christ is God's Son, our Lord and Savior. We live in our journeys of faith in fellowship with Jesus, and with his other disciples—in the church. We serve the world and all its people because we are followers of Jesus. As the former Archbishop of Canterbury Rowan Williams puts it, "Professing commitment to Jesus as Lord connects us not only to Jesus but to one another in a new way."[21] We serve others because we are part of the "body of Christ" (1 Cor 12:27). We live out our ministries in the company of the committed, those who have also heard the call of Jesus and have "got up and followed him" (Mark 2:14).

Do we hear the voice of Jesus calling us? Will we rise up and follow him? Do we know what is means to be *j*oined with Jesus, to *o*bey Jesus, to *y*ield to Jesus—so we have J-O-Y, joy in the journey of faith as we follow Jesus? Are we connected to Jesus as someone who is going somewhere? Is Jesus making us more interested in the future than the past? Does Jesus give you the norm and standard by which you test your living? Is Jesus helping you *set* your goals in life: focused on Christ, serving Christ, serving others, living in the church as disciples of Jesus Christ?

God grant that all of us will hear the voice of Jesus, saying, "Follow me."

---

21. Williams, *On Christian Theology*, 172.

2 The Church Reformed and Always Being Reformed according to the Word of God

When we think about the church, we remember its past, experience it in the present, and contemplate its future. We capture these dimensions in the phrase "the once and future church."

This is a broad topic. It's like Ernest Campbell used to say about when a pastor was told it was time to submit the sermon topic to the local newspaper. If the pastor had not yet had a rendezvous with the Holy Spirit that week for the sermon topic, the pastor would say: "Tell them the topic is the kingdom of God." This was a topic, the pastor knew, that could draw in almost any content under its umbrella! So with the "once and future church."

The "once" church can mean anything about the church in the past; the future church—that's coming, and is emerging right now in the churches of Jesus Christ throughout the world and the churches you serve on a daily basis. The church of the past is always subject to renewed looks and historical revisions of our understandings about what went on "somewhere, back there"—in the far reaches of history. The church of the future, the church to come, who knows what that will mean or be like? It is what we all hope to live into, even as the church's "shape" or "form" will be in the process of emerging.

But I hope the theme is not completely up for grabs. We can say some things about the church's past—the past of the "holy catholic church"; the past of the Reformation churches, including Reformed churches; and the past of the Presbyterian Church (U.S.A.). We can look into what we—together—see as emerging directions, today—toward the future. What directions our discussions will go, who can tell?

We can look at past, present, and future in light of some historical considerations that can provide some helpful directions or ways we can understand the church as it is emerging today and moving toward the future. We can do this in relation to some fundamentals or basics of ecclesiology, the doctrine of the church.

Here is an orienting perspective. This is the Reformed motto: "The Church Reformed and Always Being Reformed according to the Word of God." This is a slogan we often hear in relation to Presbyterian and Reformed churches. It emerges out of Reformation insights. It is basic both to our ecclesiology as Reformed Christians; as well as more widely to our theological vision itself. We can look at this slogan in relation to three phrases from the Apostles' Creed. These are three elements we confess every time we recite the creed. They deal with ecclesiology, set in the context of the whole Creed itself. The three phrases are: "I believe in the Holy Ghost, the holy catholic church, the communion of saints."

These set ecclesiology in the context of the work of the Holy Spirit in the creed itself. This ancient terminology is always in need of fresh interpretation, interpretation that seeks to understand historic meanings, as well as interpretations that can point the way to future belief and practice for the church.

More than ever, we are all finding our way together toward God's future in the church, especially in the Presbyterian Church (U.S.A.). My hope is that by looking at some of the basics of ecclesiology we can gain a sense of what has been considered important as the church has thought about itself, theologically. These perceptions can provide helps in orienting us toward the future. In what ways can we maintain continuities with the convictions of the past in relation to what is considered most important to confess about ecclesiology—while we consider these insights in light of the current—and perhaps future—contexts in our denomination? Let us consider these questions.

Reformation *was a movement, became an institution*

The Latin phrase *ecclesia reformata, semper reformanda* is of uncertain origin. It is usually translated "the church reformed and being reformed," with the added phrase, "according to the Word of God."

Sometimes the phrase has been rendered, "the church reformed and always reforming." But the better understanding is the passive—"being reformed." The proviso "according to the Word of God "gives the criterion or standard by which the reform of the church should occur.

When we hear the word "reformed" or the words "being reformed," we may think first of all about the Protestant Reformation of the sixteenth century. Our Reformed theological tradition emerged from the magisterial Reformation in Europe. The year 2017 marks five hundred years since the German monk Martin Luther (1484–1546), according to the story, nailed his Ninety-Five Theses on the door of the church in Wittenberg, Germany, on October 31, 1517. These were Luther's considered opinions about where the Roman Catholic Church had been going astray in its beliefs and practices. Luther based his critiques on his reading and interpretation of the Bible.

Luther and others who came after him became known as Protestant Reformers. They wanted to reform the Church on the basis of Scripture and to rediscover essential biblical, especially New Testament emphases on salvation: *sola gratia* (by grace alone), *sola fide* (by faith alone), *solus Christus* (by Christ alone), all on the basis of *sola Scriptura* (Scripture alone). They were called reformers, and more broadly the whole reform movement we now know as the Protestant Reformation.

But the Latin term *reformation* had a long history before Luther and company. The word is in classical Latin and there "in its broadest sense, it means every attempt to renew the essence of a community, institution, or similar group by reaching back to its originals, its primal sources."[1] By the early fifth century, the term was used with a specifically religious meaning. By the Middle Ages, within the Western monastic tradition, there were various movements for reform. The monastic tradition needed reforms at points, as does Christianity itself.

In the following centuries, various other reform movements emerged, each with a different view of what *reformation ecclesiae*, the reform of the church, should mean. We could mention various church councils and in the late Middle Ages, the efforts of the Lollards (followers of John Wyclif) and the Hussites (followers of Jan Hus), who challenged the contemporary church to be true to the Word of God. The humanist movements of Rudolph Agricola, Erasmus, and others sought a church true to a biblical vision of renewal. So currents were swirling. Reforms looked back to a pristine early church with the hope for its restoration in the present.

Luther's primary goals did not match the aims of many of his contemporaries. He was not seeking a renewal his own Augustinian order or the church's administrative apparatus. His concern for the renewal of society would be a by-product of something else. At one point, Luther said, "I have almost totally given up hope for a general reformation of the church."[2]

Only infrequently did Luther use the term "reformation" for the work he was doing. His use of the term, when he did use it, was notably different that the way others spoke of "reformation." Luther, as Emidio Campi puts it, "considered the reformation of doctrine of far greater importance than reform of practice and ritual in the church, and insisted moreover that reformation of doctrine would bring reformation of life in its wake."[3] Luther's conviction

---

1. Campi, "Reformation: A Protestant Notion?" in *Shifting Patterns of Reformed Tradition*, 16.

2. Cited in Campi, *Shifting Patterns of Reformed Tradition*, 20, from D. Martin Luthers Werke: Kritische Gesamtausgabe (Weimar: Böhlau, 1883–2009), 5:345, 20–21.

3. Ibid., 20.

was that the Word of God was primary and, as he said, "when the Word remains pure, then the life (even if there is something lacking in it) can be molded properly."[4]

The thought of Zwingli and Calvin follows Luther on this. For them, it is not a reform of church form and structure that is the focus. Their goal was not to establish a Zwinglian or a Calvinist church in itself. Their primary calls were not for a reform of church life. Rather, we can say, "They placed the Word of God at the epicentre because the church lives in relation to this alone."[5] It was this that fueled their confession of the church that is "holy and apostolic. Their understanding of this ecclesiological statement was shaped by how the church is constituted by the divine *Verbum*" (Word). Zwingli's successor, Heinrich Bullinger—the author of The Second Helvetic Confession—put it this way: "For the Church does not judge according to its own pleasure, but according to the sentence of the Holy Spirit and the order and rule of the Holy Scriptures."[6]

This is seen especially in Calvin's treatise, *The Necessity of Reforming the Church*, a piece written to Emperor Charles V in 1543. In this writing, Calvin wanted to "plead in defence both of sound doctrine and of the Church."[7] Calvin said, we all see that the "present condition of the Church is "very miserable and almost desperate." He wants to address all who "so earnestly deplore the present corruption of the Church, that they are unable to bear it any longer, and are determined not to rest till they see some amendment."[8] Calvin says that "we are accused of rash and impious innovation, for having ventured to propose any change at all in the former state of the Church." He claimed that "when God raised up Luther and

---

4. Ibid., 20, from *D. Martin Luthers Werke: Kritische Gesamtausgabe Tischreden* (Weimar: Böhlau, 1912–1921), 1:295, 3.

5. Campi, *Shifting Patterns of Reformed Tradition*, 21.

6. Bullinger, "Of the Holy Catholic Church" in Bromiley, ed., *Zwingli and Bullinger*, 323.

7. Calvin, *Necessity of Reforming the Church* in Calvin, *Calvin: Theological Treatises*, 184.

8. Ibid., 185.

others, who held forth a torch to light us into the way of salvation, and on whose ministry our churches are founded and built, those heads of doctrine in which the truth of our religion, those in which the pure and legitimate worship of God, and those in which the salvation of men are comprehended, were in a great measure obsolete."[9] So Calvin went on to give an exposition of the emerging faith of the Protestant Reformers, arguing that the Reformers "have done no small service to the Church in stirring up the world as from the deep darkness of ignorance to read the Scriptures, in laboring diligently to make them better understood, and in happily throwing light on certain points of doctrine of the highest practical importance."[10] Calvin's focus was on the two points he believed were being obscured or lost by the Roman Church: legitimate worship of God, and the ground of salvation. For Calvin, the task was not innovation but reclamation, not introducing the new but reforming the old to what he believed was crucial for the church of his day. For him and the other Reformers, it is the return to Scripture that provides the source or norm of what the church should believe.

Ecclesia Reformata, Semper Reformanda

Now to the motto, *ecclesia reformata, semper reformanda secundum verbi dei*. "The church reformed and always being reformed according to the Word of God."

A scholarly article by Michael Bush, "Calvin and the Reformanda Sayings" is the most detailed and sustained discussion of the origins of this phrase and its import.[11] He sees the expression as being of more recent origin than Reformation time, given impetus by Edward A. Dowey Jr. of Princeton Theological Seminary as well as some currency by Karl Barth and Hans Küng. But be that all as it may with the historical sources, this phrase does capture

9. Ibid., 185–86.
10. Ibid., 186–87.
11. Michael Bush, "Calvin and the Reformanda Sayings," in *Calvinus sacrarum literarum interpres*, 285–99.

some essentials of ecclesiology for churches in the Reformed theological tradition.

Over a decade ago, theologian Anna Case-Winters of McCormick Theological Seminary wrote a fine little piece on this phrase and its theological importance.[12] In it, Case-Winters says that the motto, "rightly understood, challenges both the conservative and the liberal impulses that characterize our diverse church today. It does not bless either preservation for preservation's sake or change for change's sake."

In discussing "What the motto does not mean," Case-Winters mentions the common mistranslation as "reformed and always reforming." She says, "This can mislead us to believe that the church is the agent of its own reformation. God is the agent of reformation. The church is rather the object of God's reforming work. God's agency and initiative have priority here." So the reform or reformation of the church is clearly not to be merely "change for change's sake" or the justification of any and all innovations, in and of themselves. The church is reformed by God, and its reform is to be grounded in Scripture.

This also means that the church cannot reform itself. We are reformed by the work of the Spirit of God among us since, as Case-Winters points out, "the church is God's church, a creature of God's Word and Spirit." This is basic and crucial for us. Our whole life, ongoing in the church, is based on being open and responsive to God's Word to us in Scripture and to the guidance of the Holy Spirit. This is true on the denominational level as well as on the local level. While our faith is "the faith that was once for all entrusted to the saints" (Jude 3), it is a faith entrusted to be understood and developed in accord with God's ongoing work in helping us interpret the Scriptures and "listen to what the Spirit is saying to the churches" (Rev 2:7).

---

12. Anna Case-Winters, "What Do Presbyterians Believe about 'Ecclesia Reformata, Semper Reformanda'? Our Misused Motto," in Bullock, ed., *Presbyterians Being Reformed*, xxix–xxxii. A shorter version is in *Presbyterians Today* (May 2004). This is reprinted at http://www.presbyterianmission.org/ministries/today/reformed/.

This is why as Reformed people we are open both to new expressions of our faith, as in new declarations or confessions of faith as well as to the "revisability" of our confessional understandings based on insights from Scripture and the work of the Holy Spirit. The Presbyterian Church (U.S.A.) *Book of Order*, in its discussion of confessions as subordinate standards in chapter 2 on "The Church and Its Confessional Standards," says, "The process for changing the confessions of the church is deliberately demanding, requiring a high degree of consensus across the church. Yet the church, in obedience to Jesus Christ, is open to the reform of its standards of doctrine as well as of governance. The church affirms *Ecclesia reformata, semper reformanda secundum verbum Dei*, that is, 'The church reformed, always to be reformed according to the Word of God' in the power of the Spirit."[13] (In earlier editions of *The Book of Order*, the motto was translated as "the church reformed, always reforming." Now it is better!)

At their best, our confessions themselves recognize their own limitations. They recognize there may be better ways to say what they are trying to say, and, they recognize that what they have said always stands under the judgment—and correction—of Holy Scripture. In the preface to the Scots Confession (1560), we find this:

> If any man will note in our confession any chapter or sentence contrary to God's Holy Word, that it would please him of his gentleness and for Christian charity's sake to inform us of it in writing; and we, upon our honour, do promise him that by God's grace we shall give him satisfaction from the mouth of God, that is, from Holy Scripture, or else we shall alter whatever he can proved to be wrong.[14]

The Westminster Confession indicates that "all synods or councils since the apostles' times, whether general or particular, may err, and many have erred."[15] This both concedes the fallibility of

---

13. Presbyterian Church (U.S.A.), *Book of Order 2015–2017* F.2.02.
14. Presbyterian Church (U.S.A.), *Book of Confessions*, Study Edition, 31.
15. Ibid., 6.175.

human theological declarations while also going on to say that because councils may err, "therefore they are not to be made the rule of faith or practice, but to be used as a help in both."[16]

The reform of our confessional standards, in recognition of their status as subordinate standards to Scripture, gives us foundations on which to build, and also the freedom by which to build on them. Through it all, Scripture is to be the touchstone.

The Dutch theologian G. C. Berkouwer mentioned a variation on the motto. It is, *ecclesia reformanda, quia reformata*, which being interpreted means, "because the church has been reformed, she is always in need of being reformed."[17] Berkouwer says this statement was "usually intended to indicate the Church's imperfection, parallel to the confession of believers about their imperfect lives." He mentions here two questions from the Heidelberg Catechism—one where the Catechism speaks of the small beginnings of obedience in the Christian life (Q. 114), and the other about the imperfection and defilement of "good works" (Q. 62).[18] This is reminiscent of a comment from Edward A. Dowey Jr. that reform is the institutional counterpart to repentance.[19] As permanent renovation and reformation—and repentance—is needed in the Christian life, so also in the church.

The "need to be reformed," says Berkouwer, "intends to place the Church in the revealing light of the gospel, so that there is a permanent readiness to be corrected and called back from wrong paths." When pointing out that the term "reformation" was not much used by Luther, Berkouwer went on to say that while that "reformation" concept at his time was "filled with a greatly varied content"—as we have noted with many visions of "church reformation"—it did become clear for Luther in the "concrete situation" of his own life and experience, what was needed. What Luther and

16. Ibid.

17. Berkouwer, *Church*, 183.

18. Ibid., 183.

19. Cited by Case-Winters in Bullock, ed., *Presbyterians Being Reformed*, xxxi, from Edward A. Dowey, "Always to Be Reformed" in Purdy, ed., *Always Being Reformed*, 11.

the other Reformers lodged against the contemporary Roman Catholic Church, says Berkouwer, were "accusations of abusing, neglecting, and obscuring the gospel of sovereign grace, while adding human traditions." Thus, says Berkouwer, "The Reformers called the Church back to the gospel."[20]

This highlights an aspect of "reform" on which Dowey also commented. He said, "Reform has a backward and a forward reference. It leads not only back to the Bible but also forward under the word."[21] The way forward includes the way "back." But the way "back" does not stay there, stuck in the past. The Scriptures themselves and the Holy Spirit of God also drives us forward, into the future. Anna Case-Winters captures this nicely when she writes:

> The backward and forward reference of reform invites us, on the one hand to attend respectfully to the wisdom and scriptural interpretations of those who have gone before us with humility. On the other hand, it pushes us to do more than simply reiterate what our fathers and mothers in the faith have said. Rather, we must do in our day what they did in theirs: worship and serve the living God. Therefore, while we honor the forms of faith and life that have been bequeathed to us, we honor them best in a spirit of openness to the Word and the Spirit that formed and continues to re-form the church. The church, *because of who God is*—a Living God, who loves in freedom—remains open to always being reformed.[22]

"The church reformed and always being reformed according to the Word of God."

---

20. Berkouwer, *Church*, 184.

21. Cited by Case-Winters in Bullock, ed., *Presbyterians Being Reformed*, xxxii, from Dowey, "Always to be Reformed," in Purdy, ed., *Always Being Reformed*, 10.

22. Case-Winters in Bullock, ed., *Presbyterians Being Reformed*, xxxii.

Always Being Reformed Today

What shape can this ancient motto, "the church reformed and always being reformed according to the Word of God," take for us today? Here we are in the opening act of the twenty-first century. Reformed churches, worldwide, and our own Presbyterian Church (U.S.A.) denomination have many issues and challenges with which to deal. A number of these will undoubtedly be topics of our conversations in the next days. Big churches/small churches, solo pastorates or staff positions, urban/rural settings—all the "categories" we use to define ministerial contexts and action—these all have much to face on our way to the future.

I would like to suggest three guideposts as we seek to minister and live out our vocations in God's church which is "reformed and always being reformed according to the Word of God."

First, maintain a theological openness.

This is not "openness" for the sake of openness. There are some things our minds should embrace that are basics for us. But surely we should sit loose with a number of things—those things in the church that Calvin called *adiaphora*. We maintain a theological openness because our convictions about "the church reformed" requires it.

The theologian Jürgen Moltmann has made the point that "Reformed theology is, as its name testifies, nothing other than *reformatory theology* [*reformatorische Theologie*], theology of permanent reformation."[23] Yes, says Moltmann, there is theology that began it all—the theologies emerging from the Reformation in the sixteenth century. But this is more than a "historical memory" and not just a historical commitment. Reformatory theology is "theology in the service of reformation; reformation is its historical principle. Therefore, Reformed theology is *reforming theology*. Just as the life of a Christian is, according to the first of Martin Luther's Ninety-five Theses of 1517, a 'perpetual penance,' so reformatory

---

23. Moltmann, "*Theologia Reformata et Semper Reformanda*," 120.

theology is a theology of constant turning back, the turning back to that future of God's kingdom promised by the Word of God."[24] Moltmann said that just as there is an *ecclesia reformata et semper reformanda*, there is also a *theologia reformata et semper reformanda*—theology reformed and always being reformed. In essence, said Moltmann, "'reformation according to God's Word' is 'permanent reformation'; one might say . . . it is 'an event that keeps church and theology breathless with suspense, an event that infuses church and theology with the breath of life, a story that is constantly making history, an event that cannot be concluded in this world, a process that will come to fulfillment and to rest only in the Parousia of Christ.'"[25]

Its meaning for us? Maintain a theological openness. Let your Reformed theology be a reformatory theology—open, always, to being reformed by the Word of God in Scripture, and open to considering and exploring new theological paths along your way. Not all pastors do this. One observer said he was afraid that people go to seminary to get their theology and then spend the thirty years of their ministry doing needlepoint on what they learned—and that's all! There is not always a theological inquisitiveness that marks the ranks of clergy (even some Presbyterians!). A minister who did a lot of guest preaching around the country said that when he went into the host pastor's study, he could tell what year the pastor died. The pastor died with the copyright date of the last new book the pastor bought. Reading books (and other forms of theological communication) is a way to enhance your theological inquisitiveness, to keep alive, and maintain an openness. I used to hear the great Baptist preacher Carlyle Marney say, "Theology never unpacks its bags and stays." Our Reformed theology should always be in the process of the reform that maintains a theological openness as we continue to think about things important to God, the church, and the world.

---

24. Ibid., 120–21.
25. Ibid., 121.

Second, keep a christological focus.

It is from Karl Barth that we hear repeatedly that Jesus Christ is the content of Christian theology. "For the Gospel is what it is," said Barth, "in the divine-human person of Jesus Christ Himself."[26] Indeed, at points, Barth said: "God's Word is His Son Jesus Christ. Therefore in the most comprehensive sense of the term dogmatics can and must be understood as Christology."[27] And again, "Dogmatics must actually be Christology and only Christology."[28] Jesus Christ was the focus of Barth's theology; can you think of a better focus for our own?

A christological focus should mark our Reformed theology. It is Jesus Christ to whom the Scriptures point. It is Jesus Christ who the church proclaims in preaching from the Scriptures. This is the well-known "threefold form of the Word of God," emphasized by the Reformed: Jesus Christ, the incarnate Word; Scripture, the written Word; and preaching, the Word proclaimed. The content of our proclamation is Jesus Christ, the One whom the church proclaims as "God with us."

Jesus Christ is the core of our theology. He is also the core of our ethics. What we believe and what we do should be congruent. We believe in Jesus Christ and we live and decide and serve and do all else—in obedience to Christ. Jesus is our model for living. Why? Because, as Barth said, "Jesus Christ is Himself the established kingdom of God"[29] In Jesus Christ we see the will and the way of God; we see God's kingdom in person. This is what the early church called, in Greek, *autobasileia*—a "self-kingdom." Jesus Christ is God's kingdom in himself. So he is the one who is the norm for our ethical decisions and actions. We ask ourselves, can what I decide or do be seen as consistent with Jesus Christ?

It was the Lutheran Dietrich Bonhoeffer who said about Christology, the doctrine of Jesus Christ, that the question is not,

---

26. Barth, *Church Dogmatics*, II/2, 73.
27. Barth, *Church Dogmatics*, I/2, 883.
28. Ibid., 872.
29. Barth, *Church Dogmatics*, II/2, 177.

who is Jesus Christ? as much as it is, who is Jesus Christ today? Who is Jesus Christ in the here and now? Who is Jesus Christ for us? He is the permeating presence who norms our actions and who brings salvation. What we do and what we believe—both are in Him. In an April 1928 sermon, Dietrich Bonhoeffer said, "There is no age, no moment in life when Jesus's word does not have something to say to us."[30] Jesus speaks. Will we listen?

Will we listen, and will we proclaim? Our task in the ministry of preaching is to make Jesus Christ known and to make him known intelligibly to our congregations. This involves study—both of theological sources; and of our people and our culture. This is the double hermeneutic with which preachers live. We interpret the biblical text, and we interpret the lives of our congregation. So yes, we'll read the books and participate in shared knowledge. But we will do so in order to interpret Jesus Christ in meaningful ways for the lives our folks live, day by day.

Third, sustain an ecclesiological readiness.

An ecclesiological readiness is an open nimbleness for ways our churches can experience a "being re-formed-ness" in the midst of our cultures. This doesn't mean jumping into the new for the sense of its newness. It is to be prayerful and discerning about opportunities for service to Jesus Christ that may go above and beyond our "normal ways" of carrying out our ministries. These may include new ecumenical ventures, partnerships with groups in causes dear to the heart of God such as efforts for justice, freedom, and peace, as our confessional document, the Brief Statement of Faith lists them.[31]

In the church, it is easy to settle in. To settle into the usual, the familiar, and the comfortable. These we consider as the normal activities of the Holy Spirit for us in the church. When new opportunities for "ecclesiological re-forming" come alive, we may, first of

---

30. Bonhoeffer, "God Is with Us," in *Collected Sermons of Dietrich Bonhoeffer*, 4. Bonhoeffer preached this sermon on April 15, 1928.

31. Presbyterian Church (U.S.A.), *Book of Confessions* 10.4 (line 71).

all, find the flaws, pick at the particulars, or resist the notion that our church can be "re-formed." Like that dog in the general store in West Texas mentioned earlier: "It's easier to whine than to move!" (see above p. 8) So, it is!

But sustaining ecclesiological readiness can help us look first for the opportunities, the chances for faithful witness, the potentials for the service of Jesus Christ—that new occasions can bring us. We first ask: In what ways will this help us be faithful disciples of Jesus Christ? That should be our first impulse. If we believe in a "church reformed and always being reformed by the Word of God," we should look first for the ways in which the new can enhance ministries. We look first for ways the Holy Spirit may be guiding us into "re-formed" paths.

Of course this can be upsetting at points. Marney used to say, "the new is always heresy." Obviously, we need appropriate discernment as to whether a new direction or effort is the work of the Spirit in conjunction with our study of the Word of God. Change can be unsettling. But the one thing we can say, theologically, about change is that change is God moving us from where we are to where God wants us to be. That's a stance of ecclesiological readiness.

The church being "re-formed" can be upsetting, yes. But sometimes—in the providence of God—life has to be upset in order to be set up. I've always loved the image from the Song of Moses in the book of Deuteronomy. The writer, a keen observer of nature, saw an eagle high on some lofty crag. A parent eagle will take a baby eaglet, drop it from its high nest, then swoop down to catch it and carry it to safety again. Only with this apparent cruelty does the young eaglet learn to fly. The biblical writer said: "As an eagle stirs up its nest, / and hovers over its young; / as it spreads its wings, takes them up, / and bears them aloft on its pinions, // the LORD alone guided him" (Deut 32:11,12), referring to Israel's emerging coming to life in the land. Upset to be set up.

In the providence of God, opportunities for the church to be "re-formed" may come. Be open to the Spirit and sustain an ecclesiological readiness to follow where the Spirit guides.

"The church reformed and always being reformed by the Word of God." May this ancient motto have meaning and significance for us today, as we, by God's grace, seek always to "be reformed."

3 I Believe in the Holy Ghost

I assume that most of us are well acquainted with the Holy Spirit. Pastors have at least a weekly rendezvous with the Spirit when it comes time to set the sermon title. Then there is the writing of the sermon, the preaching of it, and finally a debriefing when you and the Spirit "deconstruct" what occurred in the preaching event! Then the next week it starts again. We have more than a nodding acquaintance with the Holy Spirit!

Now we will "nod-plus" to the Spirit. We will consider the Holy Spirit in a bit of theological detail. The primary focus will come with the Spirit's activities in relation to the church.

This is the realm into which we move with the early creeds. The Apostles' Creed in its third article says, simply, "I believe in the Holy Ghost." Then follows the topics of our next two chapters: The holy catholic church; and then, the communion of saints. The Holy Spirit introduces these two phrases, which deal directly with ecclesiology. So theologically, here in the Apostles' Creed, the Spirit is related to the church. Indeed, the work of the Holy Spirit undergirds or initiates or is the foundation for the holy catholic church and the communion of saints.

The Nicene Creed has a fuller description of the Spirit's work. In the Nicene Creed, "we believe in the Holy Spirit, the Lord, the giver of life, who proceeds from the Father (and the Son), who with the Father and the Son is worshiped and glorified, who has spoken through the prophets." Then comes the description of the "one, holy, catholic and apostolic church." So the Nicene Creed provides a fuller description of who the Spirit is; the "procession" of the Spirit from the Father and the Son (in the Western church); and what the Spirit has done—"spoken through the prophets." So the Nicene Creed is a more developed and detailed account.[1]

Some dimensions of the Spirit are mentioned within these two creeds. "Some" means "a few." A "few" because the biblical witness to the person and work of the Holy Spirit is deep and extensive. Creeds and confessions through the centuries have devoted space to the Spirit as the third person of the Trinity and then discussed what the Spirit does. Theologians, of course, have written on the Spirit, so you can find a variety of treatments. Perhaps the latest "big book" on the Holy Spirit is Anthony Thiselton's *The Holy Spirit—in Biblical Teaching, through the Centuries, and Today.* It weighs in at 565 pages and pretty much covers the waterfront.[2]

Yet, how much do Reformed folks and Presbyterians think about the Holy Spirit? The phrase in the Creed is, "I believe in the Holy Ghost." Is "Ghost" too creepy so that we make it "Holy Spirit" instead? But even though there may be "friendly spirits," we Presbyterians may not pay too much attention to the Spirit; it's too amorphous, perhaps. In the early centuries, it took a while for the Spirit of God to be recognized as a full-fledged member of the Holy Trinity. The Father and Son were there—but what about the Spirit? Maybe the Spirit didn't quite measure up? Perhaps the Spirit is just a junior partner in the God corporation! But the church came around, and we have a genuine Trinity: one God in three persons: Father, Son, and Holy Spirit.[3]

Presbyterians perhaps shy away from the Spirit a bit because other denominations emphasize the Holy Spirit. Think of various holiness groups and the Pentecostals. Being "slain in the Spirit" or "speaking in tongues" after a "second baptism by the Spirit"—that's

---

1. Presbyterian Church (U.S.A.), *Book of Confessions* 1.3.

2. Thiselton, *The Holy Spirit.* Cf. Levering, *Engaging the Doctrine of the Holy Spirit;* and Kärkkäinen, ed., *Holy Spirit and Salvation.*

3. On the development of the Trinity, see McKim, *Theological Turning Points,* ch. 1.

not attractive to Presbyterians. So we may shy away from too much Spirit-talk. It is sometimes said that the Pentecostals "shout the Spirit out," the Baptists "drown the Spirit out," and the Presbyterians "freeze the Spirit out"! So we may! Maybe we come by it honestly, historically speaking. If you know well your *Book of Confessions*, you will remember that in the Westminster Confession of Faith (the great, venerable 1647 Confession that was the only doctrinal standard of our predecessor denominations here in America until 1967), the original Westminster Confession, lacked an article on the Holy Spirit. So one was added—in 1903! It only took about 256 years for the Presbyterians in America to catch up with the Spirit and add an article to the Westminster Confession that says what we believe about the Holy Spirit—the third member of the Holy Trinity! So Presbyterians have some time to make up for with the Spirit!

It is good to remember the 1984 book by Presbyterian biblical scholar Dale Bruner of Whitworth University. Along with the Lutheran theologian William Hordern, they wrote *The Holy Spirit: Shy Member of the Trinity*.[4] The Spirit may seem "shy" in our theology and church, but the Spirit is real—and active. In fact, the Reformed really do have a robust doctrine of the Holy Spirit. The Old Princeton theologian, B. B. Warfield even called John Calvin "the theologian of the Holy Spirit."[5] Yet, in a sense, this "shyness" is actually a true reflection of the New Testament itself. Thiselton mentions biblical scholars who speak of a "self-effacement" of the Holy Spirit, especially in the Synoptic Gospels. This is instead of a "self-advertisement." The Spirit comes in full force in Acts with Pentecost. In Paul's writings and in the Gospel of John (16:13, 14), the work of the Holy Spirit is portrayed as Christ-centered. The Spirit's role is, as Thiselton says, "to throw the spotlight onto Jesus Christ, or to glorify Christ."[6] So "above all," he says, "the Spirit witnesses *to Christ*."[7] The Spirit's "selflessness" points away from the

---

4. Bruner and Hordern, *Holy Spirit*.
5. Warfield, "John Calvin the Theologian," in *Calvin and Augustine*, 487.
6. Thiselton, *Holy Spirit*, 78.
7. Ibid., 374 (italics original).

Spirit to Jesus himself (John 14:26; 15:26; 16:13–14).[8] As J. E. Fison put it, the Spirit's testimony "will always be a self-effacing witness to Jesus Christ."[9] This is the witness of the Holy Spirit—a witness that continues today, right now.

The Work of the Holy Spirit

It would be too much, of course, to try to encompass the work of the Holy Spirit in one chapter, here. But there are several emphases that have been particularly strong in our Reformed tradition; and we should also consider the relationship of the Holy Spirit and the church. Let's start with several *i*'s. These relate to Scripture and the life of faith in Jesus Christ. What we will find is that there are theological realities related to God's Holy Spirit that we confess and may pretty much take for granted. The Spirit is there and is operative, always at work—but we may not give too much attention to what the Spirit has done and is continuing to do.

Inspiration

Throughout the Bible, we find instances of the Spirit of God coming upon people to equip them for certain tasks—speaking and doing. When the Christian church developed the canon of Scripture it understood biblical statements such as 2 Tim 3:16—"All scripture is inspired by God and is useful for teaching, for reproof, for correction, and for training in righteousness;" and 2 Pet 1:21—" no prophecy ever came by human will, but men and women moved by the Holy Spirit spoke from God" to apply to all the church's canonical Scripture, both Old and New Testaments. In these two passages, "inspired by God" and prophecy coming from those "moved by the Holy Spirit" link the Holy Spirit and inspiration.

So began the church's long reflections about the issues involved in speaking of the Holy Spirit and inspiration. The

---

8. Welker, *God the* Spirit, 222–23; and Welker, "Holy Spirit," 18.

9. Fison, *Blessing of the Holy Spirit*, 93, cited in Thiselton, *Holy Spirit*, 78.

questions thronged: How did the Spirit inspire people? What does a confession of the Spirit's inspiration mean in relation to the biblical authors' freedom of expression? Or, how does a confession of divine inspiration relate to the humanness of Scripture? These questions and many others surround, say, John Calvin's comment on 2 Tim 3:16: "The prophets did not speak of themselves, but as organs of the Holy Spirit uttered only that which they had been commissioned from heaven to declare."[10] Or, the end result as put by the Westminster Confession of Faith when it indicates that all the canonical books of Scripture are "given by inspiration of God, to be the rule of faith and life."[11]

They say that in preaching, the preacher's sermon should not raise more snakes than she can kill (in twenty minutes!). We cannot kill all snakes relating to the issue of the inspiration of Scripture, or how it has been understood by the Reformed or in the PC(U.S.A.). We can, however, contrast the formulation of the Westminster Confession with the Confession of 1967, which uses the language of "witness": "The one sufficient revelation of God is Jesus Christ, the Word of God incarnate, to whom the Holy Spirit bears unique and authoritative witness through the Holy Scriptures, which are received and obeyed as the word of God written. The Scriptures are not a witness among others, but the witness without parallel."[12] Here, the Holy Spirit is mentioned: the Spirit bears witness to Jesus Christ, and the Scriptures are "the word of God written" and "the witness without parallel." So, lots of images are here to sort out![13]

What's important is simply to acknowledge the role of the Holy Spirit in the origination of the Scriptures—however you want to understand that or "slice the pie." The Spirit was operative, along with human writers, to bring forth the Holy Scriptures, which the

---

10. Calvin, *Second Epistle of Paul to the Corinthians, and the Epistles to Timothy, Titus and Philemon*, 330—on 2 Tim 3:16.

11. Presbyterian Church (U.S.A.), *Book of Confessions* 6.002.

12. Ibid., 9.27.

13. On these and other matters about Scripture, especially in the Reformed theological tradition, see Rogers and McKim, *Authority and Interpretation of the Bible*.

Christian church—and our Reformed churches—acknowledge (somehow!) to be authoritative for the church's faith and practice. So the Spirit has worked in "inspiration."

Interpretation

But the Spirit isn't finished. As the Spirit was active in inspiration, so the Spirit is also active in interpretation.

One of the basics of Protestant theology is that Word and Spirit go together. Calvin spoke of this inseparability when he wrote that

> For by a kind of mutual bond the Lord has joined together the certainty of his Word and of his Spirit so that the perfect religion of the Word may abide in our minds when the Spirit who causes us to contemplate God's face, shines; and that we in turn may embrace the Spirit with no fear of being deceived when we recognize him in his own image, namely, in the Word.[14]

The Word of God in Scripture needs the Spirit to bring it alive; the Spirit witnesses or testifies to the Word as having come from God. And, says Calvin of the Word of God: "if through the Spirit it is really branded upon hearts, if it shows forth Christ, it is the word of life [cf. Phil. 2:16]."[15]

This is what we want as we read Scripture, isn't it: for the Word of God to be "really branded" upon our hearts by the Holy Spirit so the Word "shows forth Christ"? We should always ask for the guidance of the Spirit as we read, preach, or interpret Scripture. It is the Spirit who energizes the Word, applies the Scriptures to our hearts and lives, and "shows forth Christ" as the "word of life" in the here and now. So, in worship, we often have a prayer of illumination prior to the reading of Scripture and proclamation of God's Word in the preaching of the sermon.

---

14. Calvin, *Institutes* 1.9.3.
15. Ibid.

I Believe in the Holy Ghost

In our ongoing interpretation of Scripture, we should also be aware of the need to invoke the Spirit to aid in interpretation. A quick prayer for the Spirit doesn't automatically guarantee a right reading or interpretation and understanding of a Scripture passage. It isn't that easy! In the Reformed tradition there has always been an emphasis on using the best resources and tools we have to help with biblical interpretation. That's why the pastor can't stop buying books! "Teaching elders" are to have a seminary education to help them learn about interpreting Scripture. We are to crack the tough issues of Scripture with all the intelligence and resources we can gather. Yet, through it all—even with our seminary educations and our many books—what is also needed for the church as a whole and for all of us as biblical interpreters—is this reliance on the Holy Spirit as a guide to interpreting Scripture. In the broadest sense, this means, as Calvin commented on John 5:39: "The Scriptures should be read with the aim of finding Christ in them. Whoever turns aside from this object, even though he wears himself out all his life in learning, will never reach the knowledge of the truth."[16] The Holy Spirit works in biblical interpretation.

Illumination

We spoke of the prayer of illumination to ask for the Spirit's presence and help in hearing and interpreting the Word of God in Scripture. The work of the Holy Spirit in illumination is also used to describe the Spirit's work, particularly in establishing faith in Jesus Christ and in Scripture as the Word of God.

People sometimes reflect on what it is that brings us to faith in Christ, or to believe the Scriptures are the Word of God. Is it rational arguments—logical proofs for God's existence as a first step? Is it rigorous study of various philosophies that are ultimately found wanting? Is it the persuasive arguments of a friend? Many causes for faith or reasons for faith can be imagined.

---

16. Calvin, *Gospel according to St. John: Part One*, 139—on John 5:39.

THE CHURCH

Our own experience confirms that people come to the Christian faith in various ways. Perhaps some have or will come to faith in Christ in the ways mentioned. But regardless of the specific *means* that might be factors, one thing the Reformed have always maintained about the origins of faith in our lives is that faith is a work of the Holy Spirit, who illuminates our hearts and minds to confess Jesus Christ as our Lord and Savior. As Paul put it, "Therefore I want you to understand that no one speaking by the Spirit of God ever says 'Let Jesus be cursed!' and no one can say 'Jesus is Lord' except by the Holy Spirit" (1 Cor 12:3). Faith comes as a gift of God by the work of the Holy Spirit. No faith, no confession; no Spirit, no faith.

Calvin was strong on this point. He saw that "faith is the principal work of the Holy Spirit."[17] Calvin says Paul shows "the Spirit to be the inner teacher by whose effort the promise of salvation penetrates into our minds, a promise that would otherwise only strike the air or beat upon our ears." Faith itself, he goes on to say "has no other source than the Spirit." Calvin gives us a graphic image. Citing 2 Cor 3:6, Calvin says that "Paul so highly commends the 'ministry of the Spirit' [II Cor. 3:6] for the reason that teachers would shout to no effect if Christ himself, inner Schoolmaster, did not by his Spirit draw to himself those given to him by the Father [cf. John 6:44; 12:32; 17:6]."

Of all the works of the Holy Spirit, illuminating our whole selves to receive the person of Jesus Christ by faith—this is the chief or principal work the Spirit does. Quite a job description! The Spirit of God is the way that the means of salvation—faith in Jesus Christ—is given as a gift to those who believe (whom Calvin will call the "elect" of God"). Concisely, Calvin said, "Paul, in speaking of cleansing and justification, says that we come to possess both, 'in the name of . . . Jesus Christ and in the Spirit of our God' [1 Corinthians 6:11]. To sum up, the Holy Spirit is the bond by which Christ effectually unites us to himself."[18]

---

17. Calvin, *Institutes* 3.1.4.

18. Ibid., 3.1.1.

So the Spirit illuminates our lives to convey the gift of faith in Jesus Christ. At the same time, the Spirit also illuminates us to recognize that the Scriptures are God's Word to us. Again, Calvin writes, "the highest proof of Scripture derives in general from the fact that God in person speaks in it."[19] There are numerous arguments, Calvin said, that might convince us of what Scripture is—logical proofs, "rational proofs" from history. But Calvin hangs his hat on his belief that "we ought to seek our conviction in a higher place than human reasons, judgments, or conjectures, that is, in the secret testimony of the Spirit." This is sometimes called the "inner witness of the Holy Spirit" to the truth of Scripture. For Calvin, "the testimony of the Spirit is more excellent than all reason. For as God alone is a fit witness of himself in his Word, so also the Word will not find acceptance in men's hearts before it is sealed by the inward testimony of the Spirit. The same Spirit, therefore, who has spoken through the mouths of the prophets must penetrate into our hearts to persuade us that they faithfully proclaimed what had been divinely commanded."

The Scriptures are "self-authenticated" [Greek: *autopiston*]. That is, the Scriptures witness to themselves as God's Word. We recognize this by the work of the Spirit. Calvin said,

> Let this point therefore stand: that those whom the Holy Spirit has inwardly taught truly rest upon Scripture, and that Scripture indeed is self-authenticated; hence it is not right to subject it to proof and reasoning. And the certainty it deserves with us, it attains by the testimony of the Spirit. Therefore, illumined by his power, we believe neither by our own nor anyone else's judgment that Scripture is from God; but above human judgment we affirm with utter certainty (just as if we were gazing upon the majesty of God himself) that it has flowed to us from the very mouth of God by the ministry of men.[20]

---

19. Ibid., 1.7.4.
20. Ibid., 1.7.5.

So, in sum, for Calvin, "Scripture will ultimately suffice for a saving knowledge of God only when its certainty is founded upon the inward persuasion of the Holy Spirit."[21]

The importance of this work of illumination of the Spirit to Christ and to the Scriptures is that it is only by the Spirit that Jesus Christ will mean anything to us, or that the Scriptures will mean anything to us. We do not come to faith by ourselves, either in Christ, or in Scripture as the Word and truth of God. We need the work of the Spirit to make these things happen. The nineteenth-century Dutch theologian Herman Bavinck put it this way: "The objective revelation in Scripture must be completed in subjective illumination which is the gift of the Holy Spirit."[22] Bavinck echoed Calvin when he wrote that "the Holy Spirit who gave us Scripture also bears witness to that Scripture in the hearts of believers" and "it is the Spirit of God alone who can make a person inwardly certain of the truth of divine revelation."[23] To put it together, Bavinck wrote that "faith . . . reaches out in a single act to the person of Christ as well as to Scripture. It embraces Christ as Savior and Scripture as the Word of God."[24]

Indwelling

We owe our faith—in Jesus Christ and in Scripture as conveying God's Word to us—to the Spirit's illuminating work. It is the Spirit who unites us by faith with Jesus Christ. We can add a fourth *i* to the work of the Spirit, and talk about the "indwelling" of the Spirit, the Spirit who witnesses to our adoption as the children of God. As Paul says, "Do you not know that you are God's temple and that God's Spirit dwells in you?" (1 Cor 3:16). As Calvin commented, this is the way God communicates God's self to us, and the "chain" by which we are bound to God; that is, God's "pouring into us

---

21. Ibid., 1.8.13.
22. Bavinck, *Reformed Dogmatics*, 16.
23. Ibid., 21, 132.
24. Ibid., 128.

the power of His Holy Spirit."[25] The Holy Spirit is the source of our sanctification, our growth in faith: God within us. It is within sanctification where, theologically, we specially see the work of the Spirit. The Holy Spirit is active in the sanctification of Christian believers—of all Christian believers.

This moves us into the realm of the church. As the Spirit illuminates sinners and gives the gift of faith (in *regeneration* and *justification*, to use theological terms), so the Spirit of God calls together all Christian believers into the church of Jesus Christ. We will look at two aspects of the church in the next couple chapters. These are from the Apostles' Creed: "I believe in the holy catholic church," and I believe in "the communion of saints." But to conclude by considering the Holy Spirit and the church, there are three important dimensions of the Holy Spirit's work in relation to the church. These are drawn—and modified a bit—from Karl Barth.

The Holy Spirit and the Church

In the chapter on the Holy Spirit added to the Westminster Confession, the Confession says, "By the indwelling of the Holy Spirit all believers being vitally united to Christ, who is the head, are thus united one to another in the Church, which is his body."[26] Our union with Christ by faith is by the work of the Holy Spirit who also, then, unites believers with one another in the church, which is the body of Christ. So we see here the Spirit's vital action in ecclesiology.

Karl Barth treated the doctrine of the church in his large volumes on the doctrine of reconciliation. This is what we can call the subjective side of the act of reconciliation—which Barth sees as having taken place in Jesus Christ. Here, in the church, in ecclesiology, by the work of the Holy Spirit, a new community—the church—takes shape. We can say too, as Barth does, that this

---

25. Calvin, *First Epistle of Paul the Apostle to the Corinthians*, 79—on 1 Cor 3:16.

26. Presbyterian Church (U.S.A.), *Book of Confessions* 6.186.

becomes "the subjective realization of the atonement."[27] That is, the church marks the place or the body or the people, if you will, who have responded—in faith, by the work of the Holy Spirit—to the death of Jesus Christ as being the atonement for human sin, thus, reconciling us to God.

Barth discusses the Holy Spirit and the church in three ways that are helpful for us as we focus on essentials of ecclesiology.

The Holy Spirit Awakens the Community

Barth sees the church this way: "The community is the earthly-historical form of existence of Jesus Christ himself."[28] Christ is the head of this body. "It belongs to Him, and He belongs to it," said Barth, and even more strongly: "Because He is, it is; it is, because He is."[29] This is visible, says Barth, "only to faith."

Faith, comes by the Holy Spirit. So the Spirit activates or awakens the community of faith. Barth quoted Luther: "The Holy Spirit has called me by the Gospel, enlightened me with His gifts, sanctified and maintained me in a right faith, as He calls and gathers and enlightens the whole of Christendom, keeping it to Jesus Christ in the true and only faith."[30] It has to be the Holy Spirit who enlightens us, gives us faith and "calls and gathers" the community together because, as Barth says, humans are "sinful, proud and fallen," and have "neither arm, nor hand, nor even a finger to do it" for themselves. Humanity "as such is neither willing nor able to participate actively in the divine act of reconciliation."[31] This is the Reformed view of salvation: sinful humans cannot save themselves; our salvation comes from God's gracious love by the work of the Holy Spirit, who gives the gift of faith.

---

27. Barth, *Church Dogmatics*, IV/1, 643.
28. Ibid., 663.
29. Ibid.
30. Ibid., 645.
31. Ibid.

I Believe in the Holy Ghost

Since sinners cannot save themselves, Barth says it must be by "a particular awakening power of God" that humans are "born again" to participate in salvation. This "awakening power" of God, says Barth, is the Holy Spirit. The Spirit draws the community together as a "living community of the living Lord Jesus Christ in the fulfillment of its existence."[32] The Barth scholar John Thompson put it this way: The Holy Spirit is "the power of Jesus Christ in which Christ becomes ours and we become his in a living community of faith. It is God and humanity together in this way as community that is the Church and this is due to the power of the Holy Spirit awakening dead sinners to living faith and obedience."[33] So the church as we know it[34] is the work of God's Spirit, who has awakened sinners (the elect, if you will) to faith in Jesus Christ. This immediately makes the church unique among all the other institutions we know. None other have—or can claim—a divine origin like this!

The Holy Spirit Upbuilds the Community

The awakening of the community in Jesus Christ is supported by the ongoing work of the Holy Spirit in the upbuilding of the community of faith. Barth puts it this way: the Christian community continues only as the Holy Spirit sanctifies people and their "human work, building up them and their work into the true Church." The Spirit does this "in the time between the resurrection and the return of Jesus Christ and therefore in the time of the community."[35]

This, of course, is the time of the church, now. As the Spirit upbuilds the church, people are brought into active communion with God in Christ, through faith. They are brought into communion (*koinōnia*) with each other (in the communion of saints), and thus they live out their vocations or calling as disciples of

---

32. Ibid., 652.

33. Thompson, *Holy Spirit in the Theology of Karl Barth*, 93.

34. In its "earthly-historical form of existence of Jesus Christ himself" (Barth, *Church Dogmatics*, IV/1, 661).

35. Ibid., IV/2, 617. Cf. ibid., IV/1, 725.

Jesus Christ. Barth stresses the kind of "ontological connection" between Christ, the community, and the world. We are related in the deep cores of our being. Our work as disciples of Jesus Christ is carried out because Christ works in us and through us, by the ongoing, upbuilding power of the Holy Spirit. In no other way or place do we have this kind of sanction and command to live and work in these ways. As we worship and serve, it is the Spirit who enables all things as a witness to Jesus Christ.

This work of the Spirit takes shape despite the weakness, frailty, and, yes, sinfulness of those united with Jesus Christ by faith in the community of the Spirit. Our weakness may, in some sense, obscure or hide the work of the Spirit. Yet it is God's power that is made perfect in weakness, as Paul found (2 Cor 12:9). We live by faith. In the community of the Holy Spirit, our faith takes its origin from the Spirit's work, and it takes its courage from the Spirit's work, trusting that God can use the likes of us, ragtag bunch that we are. God uses us in our weakness, our sinfulness, to do Christ's work in this world—in the power of the Holy Spirit. This is our greatest hope and our continuing help. For this we are profoundly grateful.

The Holy Spirit Sends the Community

As the church proclaims the message of God's love in Jesus Christ, by the power of the Holy Spirit, the church participates in the mission of God in this world.

The Presbyterian Church (U.S.A.) *Book of Order* begins in "The Foundations of Presbyterian Polity" with a chapter on "The Mission of the Church," with the first topic being, God's Mission."[36] Jesus Christ is the head of the church, and "the Church's life and mission are a joyful participation in Christ's ongoing life and work" (F.1.0201). Christ calls and equips the church, says *The Book of Order*: "Christ calls the Church into being, giving it all that is necessary for its mission in the world, for its sanctification, and for

---

36. Presbyterian Church (U.S.A.), *Book of Order 2015–2017* F.1.01.

its service to God. Christ is present with the Church in both Spirit and Word. Christ alone rules, calls, teaches, and uses the Church as he wills" (F.1.0202).

Earlier, the Confession of 1967 had spoken of Jesus Christ as "present in the church by the power of the Holy Spirit to continue and complete his mission,"[37] which is "God's message of reconciliation" and "the sharing of God's labor of healing the enmities which separate people from God and from each other."[38] The Confession says that "wherever the church exists, its members are both gathered in corporate life and dispersed in society for the sake of mission in the world."[39] This echoes Barth's words in his long section on "The Holy Spirit and the Sending of the Christian Community" that "the true community of Jesus Christ is the community which God has sent out into the world in and with its foundation. As such it exists for the world."[40]

This is the message to share in the church and with our members. By the power of the Holy Spirit, as members of the Christian community, we are sent into the world, for the sake of the world to share the message of God in Christ—in word and deed. The church's mission is not a great, grandiose work to grab all the headlines on CNN. The church's mission is the Holy Spirit's continual awakening, upbuilding, and sending of ordinary people into the world to witness to Jesus Christ. The Confession of 1967 puts it in very down-to-earth fashion for us: "The church disperses to serve God wherever its members are, at work or play, in private or in the life of society. Their prayer and Bible study are part of the church's worship and theological reflection. Their witness is the church's evangelism. Their daily action in the world is the church in mission to the world."[41] Imagine, again: the Holy Spirit sending us and our congregations into work and play in private and in the life

---

37. Presbyterian Church (U.S.A.), *Book of Confessions* 9.07.
38. Ibid., 9.31.
39. Ibid., 9.35.
40. Barth, *Church Dogmatics*, IV/3/2, 768.
41. Presbyterian Church (U.S.A.), *Book of Confessions* 9.37.

of society to participate as the church "in mission to the world"! Breathtaking!

This is the Holy Spirit's sending of the Christian community. On a personal level as well, as Hans Küng said, "The Spirit is . . . the earthly presence of the glorified Lord."[42] The Holy Spirit makes Jesus Christ present in the here and now. The Spirit makes Jesus Christ our eternal contemporary. Ernest Campbell put it this way:

> If you have ever seen someone in need and rushed on by, intent on your own agenda—you've been with the Priest and the Levite. If you've ever reflected on the reality of evil and your own participation in it—you've been to the Upper Room. If you've ever agonized in prayer on the eve of a make or break, life or death situation—you've been to Gethsemane. If you've ever betrayed a trust, been unfaithful to a friend for personal profit—you've been with Judas to Akaldema [The Field of Blood]. If you've ever been tortured in spirit and faulted for a wrong you did not do—you've been to Golgotha. If you've ever left a situation discouraged, dejected and then been surprised by joy—you've been on the Emmaus road. If you've ever been grasped by the universality of Jesus Christ and found that all your achievements, your status, your pride of race has melted away like the snow in the sun—you've been with Paul on the road to Damascus.[43]

The Holy Spirit makes Jesus Christ real, right here in the now. "I Believe in the Holy Ghost."

---

42. Küng, *Church*, 166.

43. Adapted from Campbell, "Christian Way of Seeing," 3.

4 I Believe in the Holy Catholic Church

"I believe in the holy catholic church." This is the sparse statement of the Apostles' Creed about the church. It occurs immediately after the affirmation: "I believe in the Holy Ghost." This indicates "the holy catholic church" is an expression of the work of the Holy Spirit among the people of God. So ecclesiology is grounded in pneumatology, or as among the activities of the Holy Spirit.

The Nicene Creed, as we mentioned, describes the church as the "one holy catholic and apostolic church," expanding the marks of the church to four. But to find our way through four marks, I'd like to use the Apostles' Creed's rubric of "the holy catholic church" as a starting point for our discussion of church.

Before launching, here, we are clear that the usual word for "church" in the New Testament is *ekklēsia*. That is the word, though the concept or idea of "church" is present in many texts where that term is not specifically used. *Ekklēsia* is from the verb *kalein*, "to call." Its compound form *ekkalein* means "to call out." In classical Greek, a "herald" was one who summoned together the citizens of a city. This moves toward having an official connotation since people were to be called out and called together for officially sanctioned purposes.[1]

The Old Testament backgrounds here, as well as the use of the concept in the Septuagint (the Greek translation of the Old

---

1. Among many treatments of terminology for the church, see Küng, *Church*; Jay, *Church*; and Minear, *Images of the Church*.

Testament), is that the assembly that gathers is an "assembly of the Lord." This becomes a technical phrase since it is the Lord's people—the people of Israel who are called out (Deut 23:2ff.; 1 Chr 28:8; Neh 13:1; Mic 2:5). The Greek term *kuriakos* means "belonging to the Lord." (1 Cor 11:20; Rev 1:10).

The New Testament *ekklēsia* describes congregations of Christians who by their relationship are united with Jesus Christ. These congregations form the church or churches of God.[2] That is, theologically, the church gains its identity and purpose from the fact that it is a people "called by God": God is the one who summons and gathers the church. It is God who is at work in and with the church (1 Cor 12:28).

I Believe in the Holy Catholic Church

It may be that the confession, "I believe in the holy . . . church" is a confession that sticks in our craw. How can we believe this? If "holiness" is used, as it often is in our culture, to name a state of being "holy," which is defined in the dictionary as "exalted or worthy of complete devotion as one perfect in goodness and righteousness,"—if that is our definition of "holiness"—then how can we confess this about the church, or about ourselves as part of the church?[3]

Our dis-ease here comes from empirical experience. It's the empirical experience of our own hearts and our experience of church and churches. To be brutally honest, instead of believing in the "holy catholic church," the realities with which we have lived and do live would force us to have to confess: "I believe in the *not so holy local* church." If we can! The "not so holy church" is what we inhabit, along with fellow church members. And who can look at them—or ourselves!—and claim "holiness" in the dictionary sense? We've lived through too much. We've seen church politics, sinfulness, failings, weaknesses—any kind of very human

---

2. See 1 Cor 1:2; 10:32; Gal. 1:13 etc. for the singular usage; 1 Cor 11:16; 1 Thess 2:14; 2 Thess 1:4 for the plural usage.

3. *Merriam-Webster's Collegiate Dictionary*, s.v. "holy."

expressions—to drive us away from confessing the church's holiness—or our own. Maybe we feel like Linus in the Peanuts cartoon strip, who famously said: "I love mankind . . . it's *people* I can't stand!"[4] We love the church . . . It's the people of the church that are the problem. Put at its crassest, most brutal form, there's that old saying about the church: "The church is like Noah's ark. If it were not for the flood outside, we couldn't stand the smell inside!" So much for the holiness of the church!

But, of course, Webster's dictionary does not always provide us with biblical or theological understandings. In the Bible, in both Old and New Testaments, it is God alone who is holy in the sense of completely pure or perfect in goodness and righteousness.

When it comes to Christian believers in the New Testament, they are called "saints," (2 Cor 1:1; Eph 1:1; Col 1:2) who are sanctified ("made holy") in Christ Jesus (1 Cor 1:2; Phil 1:1). They are called to be saints (Rom 1:7). The examples cited so far are addresses to Christians by the apostle Paul, as they lived their lives in Corinth, Ephesus, Colossae, Philippi, and Rome. The whole church is called God's own people, God's holy nation, whom God has called "out of darkness into his marvelous light" (1 Pet 2:9).

So what to do with sinners in the midst of the church? When those who are called to be holy are decidedly, unholy—what then? This is the problem of imperfect holiness. This is, as the Roman Catholic theologian Karl Rahner indicated, "one of the most agonizing questions of ecclesiology which persistently recurs throughout the history of dogma." As he put it, the question is, "where this Church is to be found which so confidently declares itself to be a holy Church, therefore the Church illuminated by the light of God's own holiness."[5]

If you recall your church history, you'll remember that the church faced this kind of an issue in the early centuries, especially during periods of persecution. Some Christians would renounce

---

4. Schultz, *Complete Peanuts*, 5:1959–60. http://www.goodreads.com/work/quotes/53210-the-complete-peanuts-1959–1960-vol-5/.

5. Rahner, "The Church of Sinners," in *Theological Investigations*, VI, 253, cited in Berkouwer, *Church*, 344.

their faith, others would capitulate to emperor worship and make sacrifices before the image of the emperor. Should the church accept them back if they want to confess their faith again? After all, they had grievously sinned! What about clergy who sinned this way? In the Donatist controversy of the fourth century, the Donatists argued that the validity of sacraments depend on the personal worthiness and holiness of the administrator.

Through the theological work of Augustine, the church came to believe that the worthiness of sacraments and ordinations are not dependent on the personal worthiness of the one who administers them. The sacraments are God's work. They are God's work carried out, even through sinners. Even through sinful clergy. The holiness of the church is rooted in God's work, not in the holy piety of the church's members.[6]

Indeed, Augustine went on to define the church as the mystical body of Christ, the bride of Christ, and the mother of Christians. Yet, this church is a *corpus permixtum*, a "mixed company." There are true Christians in the church as well as those who are not genuine Christians, whose faith is a matter of outward show, and not the inward conviction of true faith. Noah's ark where clean and unclean animals existed together, and the parable of the Tares (Matt 12:24–30) where the wheat and chaff exist side by side until the harvest—these pointed to a holy church secured by God's power, which exists even with sinful people in the midst.

What becomes operative here is to see the holiness of the church as being totally dependent on God. Holiness also means being "set apart." It is this aspect that is most determinative in the New Testament. As Roman Catholic Hans Küng put it, "The Church is holy by being called by God in Christ to be the communion of the faithful, by accepting the call to his service, by being separated from the world and at the same time embraced and supported by his grace."[7] It is God who calls the church, by God's

---

6. On these issues, see McKim, *Theological Turning Points*, ch. 3; and Jay, *Church*, part 2.

7. Küng, *Church*, 325.

election or predestination, according to Calvin.[8] Those called and elected by God are those who, in faith, become disciples of Jesus Christ by the work of the Holy Spirit. They are the true and essential church whose election does not depend on themselves, but solely on the grace of God. This is the "invisible church" or the true church, the company of the elect, whose membership is known only to God.[9] The "visible church" is the church we see, all those who make an outward profession of faith in Jesus Christ. It is God who knows the heart and if a confession is a genuine confession of faith . . . or not. So the visible church is a *corpus permixtum*, this "mixed company"—those who truly confess faith in Christ, and those who don't. Calvin quoted Augustine on the church based on God's predestination: "In regard to the secret predestination of God, there are very many sheep without, and very many wolves within."[10]

It is not up to us to judge the holiness of the church. Those whom God has called and set apart to be holy and seek to do his will, to carry out God's mission in and through the church—they will do what they do on the basis of the work of the Holy Spirit who awakens them, upbuilds them, and sends them out into the world. As Küng says, "It is *God* who distinguishes the Church, sets it apart, marks it out for his own and makes it holy, by inner power over the hearts of [people] through his Holy Spirit, by establishing his reign, by justifying and sanctifying the sinner and thereby founding the communion of saints." "This is why," says Küng, "we do not simply believe *in* the holy Church, but [we] believe in God who makes the Church holy."[11] We believe the holiness of the church, grounded in God's good action in Jesus Christ. We believe this holiness just as we also believe in the forgiveness of sins and

---

8. Among other treatments of Calvin's views on the church, see G. S. M. Walker, "Calvin and the Church," in D. K. McKim, ed., *Readings in Calvin's Theology*, 212–30, and the fine treatment of Calvin's views in the context of his pastoral ministry in McKee, *The Pastoral Ministry and Worship in Calvin's Geneva*, 17–38.

9. See Calvin, *Institutes* 4.1.7.

10. Ibid., 4.1.8.

11. Küng, *Church*, 325.

the resurrection of the body. Calvin uses the image of the visible church as the "mother" of believers.[12] We need the church, justified sinners as we are. It is precisely because we are weak that we need the church. As Calvin put it, "our weakness does not allow us to be dismissed from her school until we have been pupils all our lives." Then he says bluntly: "It is always disastrous to leave the church." This was Calvin's warning to his readers then, and now.

Calvin was a realist about the holiness of the church. He knew full well that on this side of glory the church as it is—the "not so holy local church"—is "at the same time mingled of good men and bad."[13] It's like when Oliver Cromwell had his portrait painted. The painter wanted to flatter the Lord Protector. But when the painting was unveiled, Oliver Cromwell shouted at the painter, words to the effect: "Mr. Lesley, paint me warts and all!" The visible church does have "warts and all." But this is what God has established here in the midst of history. For Calvin, "if the Lord declares that the church is to labor under this evil—to be weighed down with the mixture of the wicked—until the Day of Judgment, they are vainly seeking a church besmirched with no blemish." Wickedness and scandal are no justifications for leaving the church. Ultimately, Calvin said, "separation from the church is the denial of God and Christ."[14]

So the visible church is a mixed bag. The visible church is where the Holy Spirit is at work in sanctification, the process of "making holy." As Küng points out, in the New Testament, "believers are 'saints' in so far as they are 'sanctified.' The concept of sanctification is usually passive in Paul; he speaks of those who are 'sanctified in Christ Jesus' (1 Cor 1:2) and 'sanctified by the Holy Spirit' (Rom 15:16). There are no self-made saints, only those who are 'called to be saints' (1 Cor. 1:2; Rom. 1:7; cf. 1:6; 1 Cor. 1:24)."[15] It is God's power in the Spirit that is "at work within us" (Eph. 3:20). For Calvin, this meant "the church is holy, then, in the sense

---

12. See Calvin, *Institutes* 4.1.4.
13. Ibid., 4.1.13.
14. Ibid., 4.1.10.
15. Küng, *Church*, 324–25.

I Believe in the Holy Catholic Church

that it is daily advancing and is not yet perfect: it makes progress from day to day but has not yet reached its goal of holiness."[16] How are we doing on the "daily advancing"—in our lives and churches?

Yet, in looking at the Apostles' Creed, Calvin commented that in the creed, "forgiveness of sins appropriately follows mention of the church."[17] This is due to the "imperfect holiness" issue. Forgiveness of sins is a necessary part of the church's life—and our own lives. Needless to say, for the Reformed, perfection has never been a viable possibility in the Christian life, in the way it was for other branches of the Reformation.[18] Calvin saw the claim for perfection to be an "overscrupulousness" that is "born rather of pride and arrogance and false opinion of holiness than of true holiness and true zeal for it."[19] But forgiveness of sins is part of what the church does. As Calvin says, "forgiveness of sins . . . is for us the first entry into the church and Kingdom of God. Without it, there is for us no covenant or bond with God."[20] Each of us in our Christian lives, says Calvin, knows that throughout our lives there are "many infirmities that need God's mercy."[21] So, "carrying, as we do, the traces of sin around with us throughout life, unless we are sustained by the Lord's constant grace in forgiving our sins, we shall scarcely abide one moment in the church." We should ponder that there is "pardon ever ready" for our sins and that "we must firmly believe that by God's generosity, mediated by Christ's merit, through the sanctification of the Spirit, sins have been and are daily pardoned to us who have been received and engrafted into the body of the church."[22]

In sanctification, Christian believers—and the church itself—cooperates with the Holy Spirit. We are to "grow in the grace

16. Calvin, *Institutes* 4.1.17.

17. Ibid., 4.1.20.

18. As for example in the Arminian theological tradition. See D. K. McKim, *Introducing the Reformed Faith*, 155–57.

19. Calvin, *Institutes* 4.1.16.

20. Ibid., 4.1.20.

21. Ibid., 4.1.21.

22. Ibid.

and knowledge of our Lord and Savior Jesus Christ" (2 Pet 3:18). In this dimension of the church's life, and our own, we can find ways by which we grow in holiness, in sanctification, in living out the calling through which our election in Jesus Christ is made known to us. Sanctification is not autopilot or cruise control. It's not set it and forget it. In our growth in faith and in "the grace and knowledge of our Lord and Savior Jesus Christ" (2 Pet 3:18), we have responsibilities to seek ways to grow. To grow will mean we take each letter of the word, *grow*—G-R-O-W—and recognize they mean Go Right On Working. G-R-O-W. We grow in faith and holiness by the work of God's Spirit within us and among us. We cooperate with the Spirit in seeking to be holy—giving ourselves to God's purposes for us in Jesus Christ; and growing in faith and devotion and service to Christ.[23]

To be holy does mean to be "set apart." We are "set apart" in the church by God's purposes for us. This led Hans Küng to comment about the church that "because it is holy, it must be holy; the indicative brings an imperative with it."[24] If holiness is a mark of the church, grounded in God's Spirit, then the church, as Küng writes:

> presses forward, set apart from the world, different from the other communities of the world. The Church is not like natural communities, people bound together by their way of life, like families, nations, states. Nor is it like communities of interest, like trades unions or professional associations, like economic or cultural organizations. The way of the Church must be different from those of other societies. It has a different foundation, for which there is no substitute; different means, which cannot be replaced by those borrowed from other communities; a different goal, distinct form the aims of other communities; it has a different scale of values for measuring what is important or unimportant, what should be seen as success or failure, as glory or shame; it has a different membership

---

23. See D. K. McKim, *Introducing the Reformed Faith*, 157–64.
24. Küng, *Church*, 329.

qualification, incomprehensible to outsiders—a single qualification: faith.[25]

Let us commit ourselves to the Creed's affirmation: "I believe in the *holy* catholic church."

I Believe in the Holy Catholic Church

Our Protestant sensibilities are often tested when we move on to confess faith in the "holy *catholic* church." You've perhaps been in churches where in printed versions of the Apostles' Creed, the word "catholic" has been replaced with the word "Christian." So: "I believe in the holy Christian church." According to Jürgen Moltmann, this practice reached back to Reformation times. "When, in the conflicts of the Reformation period," Moltmann writes, "'Catholic' became the party name for one particular church, the Reformers also replaced the word 'catholic' in the German creed by 'general' or 'Christian' church."[26]

When we confess the "catholicity" of the church, we inherit meanings from the past. The Greek term *katholikos* (in Latin *catholicus* or *universalis*) is related to an adverb referring to the whole, or general—"generally" or "universally." The first ecclesiastical usage was by Ignatius of Antioch who said, "Let that be considered a valid eucharist which is celebrated by the bishop, or by one whom he appoints. Wherever the bishop appears, let the congregation be present; just as wherever Jesus Christ is, there is the catholic church."[27] This means, quite clearly, the whole church, the full or complete church, in contrast to local churches—churches here and there. It is the uniting, pervasive power of Jesus Christ which is found in all the churches that gives the church its "catholicity."

---

25. Ibid., 329.

26. Moltmann, *Church in the Power of the Spirit*, 348. This was true, particularly in the Lutheran tradition.

27. Ignatius of Antioch, *Smyrn.* 8.1–2; cited in Moltmann, *Church in the Power of the Spirit*, 347–48. On this topic, see Dulles, *Catholicity of the Church*, ch. 1 and appendix B.

As time went on, the "catholic" nature of the church came to refer to the church's "spatial catholicity," the church's presence throughout the whole inhabited world—the *oikumenē*—the whole inhabited earth, the "household" of the world. The term also came to refer to the church's "temporal catholicity," that the Christian church exists throughout all periods of history. When the church in the first centuries was hammering out its faith in relation to various heretics and schismatics, the term "catholic church" also became synonymous with the term "orthodox" and the notion of orthodox faith. So the orthodox faith marked the true church—the church that is rightfully the genuine church of Jesus Christ.

Now it is clear that to speak of the "catholicity" of the church also relates us to the unity or oneness of the church. The terms are correlative. The church's unity reaches out into all times and places and so displays the church's *catholicity*. The church's catholicity is the church's unity as extended into all times and places.

The catholicity of the church can also relate to the fullness of the truth the church confesses. The apostle Paul said, "For I did not shrink from declaring to you the whole purpose of God" (Acts 20:27). The church proclaims the "whole purpose of God"—all that God has revealed to us. We do not break off certain segments, set them to the side or lift them up and absolutize them on their own as only small portions of the truth. So qualitatively the catholicity of the church can refer to the fullness of the church's message of the gospel of Jesus Christ.

Moltmann says that

> if we put the spatial and the inner meaning of the word [*catholic*] together, then the church with its inner wholeness is related to the whole of the world. This follows inevitably from its definition as the church of Christ. Being entirely related to Christ, it is related to the whole world, for whose reconciliation Christ was sacrificed by God, and for whose liberation and unification all power was given him in heaven and on earth (cf. Eph. 1.20ff.).[28]

---

28. Moltmann, *Church in the Power of the Spirit*, 348.

Think of what this may mean for the church's mission and ministries. If the church is catholic since it is united by faith to the Christ who has received all power and who "fills all in all" as Eph 1:22 says, then the church surely is related to the whole world in Jesus Christ. The church carries out Christ's purposes and mission in all things, in all places, and in all circumstances. No inch of real estate is outside the reign of Christ and thus, the church's catholicity. No human problem or situation is of "no concern" to the church because the church's catholicity reaches into the fullness of human life—the human life for whom Jesus Christ died. The ministry and message of Jesus Christ is universal, and this is what *catholikos* means: "universal." The church's ministries and message are to pervade the fullness of the created order and the human lives it embraces—universally. The church is wide and deep—the "breadth and length and height and depth" (Eph 3:18) of Jesus Christ himself. This opens ministries for us—as wide and deep as the world itself and its peoples. No truncated gospel, here! As Hans Küng put it, "A Church is never there just for itself, but by its very nature is there for others, for [hu]mankind as a whole, for the entire world."[29] Are we living out the catholicity of the church in its fullness? Into what new directions can the Spirit lead us as we confess "I believe in the holy catholic church"?

The Church Is One

As we have seen, there is a close relationship between the church's catholicity in its breadth of expression and the church's unity as one in Christ. The Nicene Creed starts with the nod toward the church's unity: "one holy catholic and apostolic church." The churches that exist throughout the world, as local worshiping bodies are expressions of the one holy catholic church.

This was the way it was from earliest times. The term *ekklēsia*, the word for "church" in the New Testament, has the basic meaning of a local community, a local church situated somewhere or

---

29. Küng, *Church*, 302.

other. But the local communities of faith we read about in the New Testament are, as Küng puts it, "only local Churches at all, inasmuch as they are the manifestation, the representation, the realization of the one *entire*, all-embracing, universal Church, of the Church as a whole. While the individual local Church is *an* entire Church, it is not *the* entire Church."[30] So the movement goes from the general to the specific—not the other way around. Individual, local congregations draw their life from the entire church of Jesus Christ, which is one. The church's unity is in Christ and, as Küng says, "by being inwardly at one in the same God, Lord and Spirit, through the same Gospel, the same baptism and sacred meal and the same faith. The total Church is the Church as manifested, represented and realized in the local Churches."[31] This echoes the words in Eph 4: "Here is one body and one Spirit, just as you were called to the one hope of your calling, one Lord, one faith, one baptism" (vv. 4–5). The church's unity is not based on ecclesiastical authority or on the voluntary association of local, autonomous community units. The church's unity is theological; and the church's unity is Jesus Christ himself. As Barth says, what unites communities separated by geography is "the Lord who attests Himself in the prophetic and apostolic word, who is active by His Spirit, who as the Spirit has promised to be in the midst of every community gathered by Him and in His name. He rules the Church and therefore the Churches. He is the basis and guarantee of their unity."[32]

John Calvin contended in his *Institutes* that as believers are "joined and knit together," so "they are made truly one since they live together in one faith, hope, and love, and in the same Spirit of God. For they have been called not only into the same inheritance of eternal life but also to participate in one God and Christ [Eph 5:30]."[33] As he put it in his *Necessity of Reforming the Church*, the principle from which Paul derives unity is, that there is "one Lord,

30. Ibid., 300.
31. Ibid.
32. Barth, *Church Dogmatics*, IV/1, 674–75.
33. Calvin, *Institutes* 4.1.2.

one faith, one baptism, one God and Father of all" who hath called us into one hope, (see Eph 4:4, 5.) Therefore, we are one body and one spirit, as is here enjoined, if we adhere to God only, i.e., be bound to each other by the tie of faith."[34] For "God invites all with His one voice, so that they may be united in the same agreement of faith, and study to help one another,"[35] Faith is the means by which the unity of the church—which is a unity with Christ—is made real. In commenting on Eph 4:5, Calvin said:

> Whenever you read this word 'one' here, understand it as emphatic, as if he said 'Christ cannot be divided; faith cannot be rent; there are not various baptisms, but one common to all; God cannot be divided into parts.' Therefore it behooves us to cultivate among ourselves a holy unity, composed of many bonds. Faith, and baptism, and God the Father, and Christ, ought to unite us, so that we coalesce, as it were, into one man [person] . . . The unity of the faith, which is here mentioned, depends on the one eternal truth of God, on which it is founded.[36]

It is in "the Church of God, where unity of faith ought to prevail."[37] The church is the locus where all believers' unity with Christ is expressed. Individual Christians are to act as "one of the flock" since the "saints" (believers) are "gathered into the society of Christ." It is "the Gospel, which ought to be the bond of unity."[38]

---

34. Calvin, *Necessity of Reforming the Church*, 167.

35. Calvin, *Epistles of Paul the Apostle to the Galatians, Ephesians, Philippians and Colossians*, 172—on Eph 4:4.

36. Ibid., 172–73—on Eph 4:5.

37. Calvin, *Acts of the Apostles* 2:160—on Acts 19:23.

38. Ibid., 4—on Acts 14:4. Calvin faulted the papists for grounding unity only in the church and not in the authority of Scripture, "as if the unity of the Church were itself founded elsewhere than on belief in Scripture" (Calvin, *Gospel according to St. John: Part Two*, 180—on John 19:24).

Church Unity as Gift and Task

While our unity in Christ is given to the church as a gift, it is also a task. This is captured by the Belhar Confession from the twentieth-century in South Africa, the most recent addition to the Presbyterian Church U.S.A.'s *Book of Confessions*. Belhar says:

> We believe in one holy, universal Christian church, the communion of saints called from the entire human family . . . We believe that unity is, therefore, both a gift and an obligation for the church of Jesus Christ; that through the working of God's Spirit it is a binding force, yet simultaneously a reality which must be earnestly pursued and sought: one which the people of God must continually be built up to attain; that this unity must become visible so that the world may believe.[39]

Our unity is Christ's gift. But it is also the obligation of the body of Christ earnestly to pursue and seek visible expressions of this unity, "so that the world may believe."

It is this unity in Christ for which Christ himself prays. In his great "high priestly prayer' in John 17, Jesus prays "that they may be one, as we are one" (John. 17:21). Calvin says that Christ

> places the end of our happiness in unity, and justly. For the ruin of the human race is that, alienated from God, it is also broken and scattered in itself. Conversely, therefore, its restoration lies in its proper coalescence in one body (*in corpus unum rite coalescat*); as Paul sees in Eph. 4.2, 16 the perfection of the Church in believers being joined together in one Spirit, and says that apostles, prophets, evangelists and pastors are given to restore and build up the body of Christ until it arrives at the unity of faith. And therefore he exhorts believers to grow into Christ, who is the Head from whom the whole body, joined together and connected by every bond of supply according to the operation in the measure of every part, makes increase of it to edification. Wherefore, whenever Christ speaks of unity, let us remember how foul and

---

39. *Book of Confessions* (2016), 10.3.

horrible is the world's scattering apart from Him. Next let us learn that the beginning of a blessed life is when we are all governed and live by the one Spirit of Christ.[40]

This unity of believers in the church in the unity of faith is a unity shared in the fellowship of the church.[41] It is a unity to "cultivate" since we Christians "all meet together to share that symbol of that sacred unity."[42] We should cherish, "as much as we can, unity with the whole body."[43] "Servants of Christ" should "take positive action to foster unity"[44] When Christians examine themselves in preparation to receive the Lord's Supper, Calvin says they must bring "faith and repentance" to the table. The imperative to work for unity is emphasized when Calvin wrote that "under repentance I include love, for there is no doubt that the man, who has learnt to deny himself in order to devote himself to Christ and His service, will also give himself whole-heartedly to the promotion of the unity which Christ has commended to us."[45] The Lord's Supper, which dramatizes the reality of unity in Christ is also the occasion in which efforts for the unity of Christians in Christ is to be expressed—as a sign of a repentance which features love as a primary component.

Calvin knew from his own experience, as well as from the New Testament letters he interpreted, ways the unity of the church can be fractured, by "heretics" as well as by others within the body of Christ itself. Yet, it is the church's duty to overcome the situations and go beyond the persons who would fracture the unity of the body of Christ and lead those in the church astray. Calvin

---

40. Calvin, *Gospel according to St. John: Part Two*, 147–48—on John 17:21.

41. Calvin said: "So powerful is participation in the church that it keeps us in the society of God" (*Institutes*, 4.1.3).

42. Calvin, *Epistles of Paul the Apostle to the Galatians, Ephesians, Philippians and Colossians*, 172—on Eph 4:5; and Calvin, *First Epistle of Paul to the Corinthians*, 217—on 1 Cor 10:17.

43. Calvin, *Acts of the Apostles*, 1:158—on Acts 6:1.

44. Ibid., 2:25—on Acts 15:2.

45. Calvin, *First Epistle of Paul the Apostle to the Corinthians*, 253—on 1 Cor 11:28.

charged that "it is for us to work hard and strive in every way to bring if possible the whole world to agree in the unity of the faith."[46] Christians must work for the unity of the church. This is an obligation for Christians from the earliest times to the present, and into the future. In contemplating the "final coming of Christ," Calvin asks, "For what is the purpose of the coming of Christ but to gather us all together in one from this dispersion in which we are now wandering? Therefore the nearer His coming is the more we must bend our efforts that the scattered may be brought together and united and that there may be one fold and one Shepherd (John 10.16)"[47]

Calvin's "devotion to 'the church,' which is reiterated with the greatest frequency" is always, wrote John T. McNeill, "a devotion to 'the catholic church' or the church of God in all her parts. Unified in the headship of Christ, she is to be extended into and beneficially operative in the whole world."[48] Famously, Calvin wrote to Archbishop Thomas Cranmer in England, who was proposing a general synod for the closer union of Reformed churches that when "the members of the Church being severed, the body lies bleeding." So much did this concern Calvin, he said, that "could I be of any service, I would not grudge to cross even ten seas, if need were, on account of it."[49] As McNeill puts it, "The idea of a catholic unity dominated the church theory of Calvin."[50]

---

46. Calvin, *Gospel according to St. John: Part One*, 262—on John 10:8.

47. Calvin, *Hebrews and I and II Peter*, 145—on Hebrews 10:25. Calvin indicated that "we who are the sheep of Christ repose in a safe place when we hold the unity of faith" (*Epistles of Paul the Apostle to the Galatians, Ephesians, Philippians and Colossians*, 329—on Col 2:8).

48. McNeill, *Unitive Protestantism*, 71. McNeill cites Calvin's commentary on Isa 55:5: "The restoration of the church may be regarded as the restoration of the whole world."

49. Calvin, Letter 294 to Cranmer, April 1552 in Calvin, *Selected Works of John Calvin*, 5:355. Cf. McNeill, *Unitive Protestantism*, 247.

50. McNeill, *Unitive Protestantism*, 217. McNeill cites other examples of Calvin's efforts toward unity. On this see also McKim, "Reformed Foundations for the Unity of the Church in the Contemporary World" in Robbins, ed., *Ecumenical and Eclectic*, 7–23.

Does this same passion for a "catholic unity" dominate our ecclesiology, today? May we come to a fuller awareness of what we confess when we say, "I believe in the holy catholic church."

5 I Believe in the Communion of Saints

As we have seen, the Apostles' Creed in its third article brings us to confess, "I believe in the Holy Ghost, the holy catholic church." The holy catholic church is the work of the Holy Spirit, as are the phrases that follow: "I believe in the Holy Ghost, the holy catholic church, the communion of saints, the forgiveness of sins, the resurrection of the body, and the life everlasting." What emerges in the holy catholic Church is cumulatively described in these phrases. In the church, we participate in the communion of saints, the forgiveness of sins, and then—in the future—the resurrection of the body and the life everlasting. This sequence deals with the here and now as well as the hereafter.

Scholars tell us that the phrase "communion of saints" (Latin: *communio sanctorum*) did not belong to the original Apostles' Creed but was added later. The Dutch theologian G. C. Berkouwer says that "the insertion of *communio* was understood as a more exact explication of *ecclesia*" (church).[1]

Behind this Latin phrase *communio sanctorum* is the Greek word *koinōnia*. We are familiar with this term, often translated "fellowship" or "communion." It is a rich term indicating our fellowship with Christ in the Holy Spirit. The term also connotes a "participation" and "sharing." This sense of participation as a "communion" is the sense in 1 Cor 1:9: "God is faithful; by him you were called into the fellowship of his Son, Jesus Christ our

---

1. Berkouwer, *Church*, 92.

I Believe in the Communion of Saints

Lord." Our fellowship is a participation in Jesus Christ, meaning, of course, a participation in faith. The word *koinōnia* also appears in the familiar benediction from 2 Cor 13:13: "The grace of the Lord Jesus Christ, the love of God, and the communion of the Holy Spirit be with all of you." Sometimes it has been translated as the "fellowship of the Holy Spirit." Our communion or fellowship is a participation in the Holy Spirit through which we receive the grace of Jesus Christ and the love of God. So *koinōnia* is a rich term, denoting a sharing, an intimacy, a deep fellowship and communion. When *koinōnia* refers to fellowship with God in Christ through the Spirit, it is about the richest term imaginable because it describes the inner life of God.

So the church, in the Apostles' Creed, is defined as a "communion of saints." But interpreting this phrase has not been easy. In the long history of the church there have been three major interpretations of the meaning of the "communion of saints." The difficulty in interpretation has come from the ambiguity of the Latin text of the Apostles' Creed. There the phrase runs: "I believe in the *sanctorum communionem*."[2] But because of the particular grammatical forms here (the genitive *sanctorum* is both masculine and neuter in ending), there are seven grammatical possibilities for translation. We will not go through each of these. (It would take the patience of a saint to endure that!) But here are three major interpretations. These have appeared at different points in the church's history. We do not have to choose absolutely or exclusively from among them. We don't have to choose one as being the only "correct" interpretation of the phrase. Each of them is a possible theological understanding. The multiplicity of views here on interpretation should not be unnerving. It opens more possibilities for us, a wider range of understandings. We can view the phrase in three different lights, through three different lenses.

There are two major divisions in the interpretations. One has been called a sacramental interpretation. The other main division

---

2. See Wandel, *Reading Catechisms*, 71.

is a personal interpretation. In the personal interpretation category, there are two main viewpoints.³

Participation in Holy Things (Sacramental)

First, the sacramental, a view quite popular in the Middle Ages. In this view, the phrase "communion of saints" has the sense of "participation in holy things." In the early church, this meant primarily, participation in the sacraments—especially in the Eucharist or Lord's Supper. The *sancta* of *sanctorum communio*, which we have translated as "saints" literally means "holy." So the phrase can be rendered "communion" or "participation in holy things" (instead of the "holy people"—or saints). In this view, the Christian is linked to eternal salvation in the church through the sacraments. This means we are confessing our belief that through the sacraments, the means of grace, God is drawing us into communion with God and is imparting to us God's own salvation and love. In the twelfth century, Peter Abelard said this communion was "that communion by which the saints are made saints, are confirmed in their sanctity, by participation in the divine sacrament."⁴

Now our views of the sacraments today are not the same as those of Abelard and medieval Catholicism. But we can see truth here in this sacramental view. We do believe sacraments—baptism and the Lord's Supper—are means of grace. They are "signs and seals" of God's promises to us in Jesus Christ, as Calvin said. Sacraments are means of nurturing faith. The Lord's Supper nourishes us as often as we receive it with the reception of the benefits of Jesus Christ in his life, death, and resurrection. Sacraments are made effective by faith. Faith is the means of our union with Jesus Christ, established in us by the Holy Spirit. In the Lord's Supper—often called communion, we experience the benefits of Christ's work by faith as we partake in faith, united with Jesus Christ. As the

3. See Benko, *Meaning of Sanctorum Communio*.
4. Abelard, *Expos. In symb. apost.* Cited in Kelly, *Early Christian Creeds*, 393.

Westminster Confession puts it, the Supper is given to the church for the "perpetual remembrance" of Christ's sacrifice in his death, "the sealing all benefits thereof unto true believers, their spiritual nourishment and growth in him."[5] So in sacraments, we participate in a unique way in "holy things." In baptism, said Calvin, "we are received into the society of the church, in order that, engrafted in Christ, we may be reckoned among God's children."[6] In the Lord's Supper, we receive Jesus Christ, who is "the only food of our soul," says Calvin. God invites us to Christ, that, "refreshed by partaking of him, we may repeatedly gather strength until we shall have reached heavenly immortality."[7] So, consider the interpretation "I believe in the participation in holy things."

Communion of Saints (Personal)

Beside the sacramental view, we have two forms of the personal view of the meaning of *sanctorum communio*.

The Church Here and Now

The first of these two views is that "communion of saints" refers to the church here and now. In this view, we are really confessing our faith in the "union of the saints." This accords with the unity and catholicity of the church, expressed in the previous phrase of the creed. As you know, in distinction from the Roman Catholic view and practice of ascribing the title "saint" to only specified, special people, the Reformation churches took the term in its New Testament sense of using "saints" in the plural, to describe all the members of a visible church in some place. We can greet one another as saints in Jesus Christ. Saints are those who are being "made holy" or "sanctified"—by the power of the Holy Spirit. Those who profess Jesus Christ as Lord and Savior participate in the work of the

---

5. Presbyterian Church (U.S.A.), *Book of Confessions* 6.161.
6. Calvin, *Institutes* 4.15.1.
7. Ibid., 4.17.1.

Holy Spirit who is upbuilding the church and is "the power at work within us" (Eph 3:20).

The New Testament uses many images to describe the church. The New Testament scholar Paul Minear in his *Images of the Church in the New Testament* lists some ninety-six of these. So there are lots of ways the church is described in Scripture. In his discussion of the image of church as "the sanctified," Minear says that in the New Testament, "wherever the church is spoken of as the saints, the power of the Holy Spirit is assumed to be at work within it. The community of saints has been born of the Spirit and baptized into this one Spirit. On this community the Spirit is poured out."[8]

So the saints, those being "sanctified," are united by faith in the community of the Holy Spirit—the church. The "communion of saints" is our "common-union" with one another in the church around Jesus Christ, by the power of the Spirit. We share our faith in Christ in common. We seek Christ's will for us in common. We live out God's mission in this world in common. "I am the vine, you are the branches," said Jesus (John 15:5). Our union and common union with Jesus Christ and with each other is expressed in the body of Christ, the church. So "I believe in the communion of saints" can be a way of confessing our faith as part of the church, here and now.

The Whole Company of God's People

But this phrase can be pushed one step farther. The third interpretation of the phrase asks us to expand our view of the church itself. Not only are we united with our sisters and brothers here around Jesus Christ in the household of faith. We are also united in time with all the Christians who have ever lived. We have a communion with these saints that is as broad and long and wide as eternity itself.

---

8. Minear, *Images of the Church in the New Testament*, 137.

I Believe in the Communion of Saints

The bishop Nicetas died around 415 and served in present-day Serbia. He is sometimes called Saint Nicetas. This dear bishop gives the oldest explanation we have for the meaning of our phrase: *sanctorum communio*, the communion of saints. He wrote:

> What is the church, but the congregation of all the saints? From the beginning of the world patriarchs, prophets, martyrs, and all other righteous persons who have lived or are now alive, or shall live in time to come, comprise the church, since they have been sanctified by one faith and manner of life, and sealed by one Spirit and so made one body, of which Christ is declared to be head, as the Scripture says. Moreover, the angels, and the heavenly virtues and powers too, are banded together in this church . . . So you believe that in this Church you will attain to the communion of saints.[9]

As the patristics scholar J. N. D. Kelly writes, "Communion of saints is here interpreted as standing for that ultimate fellowship with the holy persons of all ages, as well as the whole company of heaven, which is anticipated and partly realized in the fellowship of the Catholic Church on earth."[10]

This is the ultimate big tent, isn't it? This is a comprehensive view of the church: past, present, and future. No matter who we are—with all the artificial labels our cultures give: race, gender, sexual orientation, economic location—"we are the church, together," as the song puts it. Those who have gone before us and who are now a great company of the heavenly hosts are sisters and brothers of ours in Jesus Christ, in the church. It reminds us of the image in Heb 12:1—"We are surrounded by so great a cloud of witnesses." The nineteenth-century theologian Herman Bavinck put it crisply: "In the broadest sense, then, the church embraces all who have been saved by faith in Christ or will be saved thus."[11] This is the communion of saints—of all the saints!

Question 55 of the Heidelberg Catechism asks:

---

9. Cited in Kelly, *Early Christian Creeds*, 391.
10. Ibid.
11. Bavinck, *Reformed Dogmatics*, 599.

The Church

> Q. What do you understand by "the communion of saints"?
>
> A. First, that believers one and all, as members of this community, share in Christ and in all his treasures and gifts [1 John 1:3; 1 Cor. 1:9; Rom 8:32]. Second, that each member should consider it a duty to use these gifts readily and joyfully for the service and enrichment of the other members [1 Cor 6:17; 12:12–21; 13:5; Phil 2:4–6].[12]

In his commentary on the Heidelberg Catechism, Karl Barth recognized the problem with translating the phrase "communion of saints" in the Latin. He said, "The problem arises where whether we are to think of the *sancti* [the communion of 'holy people'] or the *sancta* [the communion of 'holy things.']." Barth believed the Heidelberg "intends both possibilities." He wrote, "The first sentence seems to point to *sancta*, the second to *sancti*." That is, the first sentence points to the communion of holy things and the second sentence to the communion of holy people. Says Barth, "Every individual Christian is given full participation in the *gift* which is Christ himself." This is where the catechism says, "believers one and all, as members of this community, share in Christ and in all his treasures and gifts." Then, says Barth, "On the other hand *each one* is called to give himself totally to serve the 'benefit and welfare of other members' and just in this way to serve the benefit and welfare of all" where the catechism says, "each member should consider it a duty to use these gifts readily and joyfully for the service and enrichment of the other members."[13]

The benefits received from Jesus Christ issue forth in the duty to use the gifts given in service to others. As Berkouwer says when talking about the fellowship of the communion of saints, "We meet here with a mutual dependency that embraces mutual service as being at the disposal of one another and as an unceasing interest in the other" (Phil 2:4: ["Let each of you look not to your own interests, but to the interests of others."]) Or, put succinctly by Paul for the community of saints in Rome: "Serve the Lord" (Rom. 12:11).

---

12. Presbyterian Church (U.S.A.), *Book of Confessions* (2016), 4.055.
13. See Barth, *Heidelberg Catechism for Today*, 87.

I Believe in the Communion of Saints

This is perhaps the best perspective for us in interpreting "the communion of saints." We know that we participate in "holy things" as a "holy people." This is our calling. This is what the Holy Spirit is doing in the church. This is what we receive and what we give. As Calvin said, "It is as if one said that the saints are gathered into the society of Christ on the principle that whatever benefits God confers upon them, they should in turn share with one another."[14]

Holy People and Holy Things

When he dealt with this phrase in his *Church Dogmatics*, Barth made a tighter connection between these two interpretations of "holy things" and "holy people." Barth wrote:

> The genitive certainly indicates that it is the communion of the *sancti*, i.e., of those who are sanctified by the Holy Spirit, of all Christians of every age and place. But it also means—and apart from this we cannot see what it is that makes them *sancti* in their human being and activity—communion in the *sancta*: the holy relationships in which they stand as *sancti*; the holy gifts of which they are partakers; the holy tasks which they are called upon to perform; the holy position which they adopt; the holy function which they have to execute. From this standpoint the *communio sanctorum* is the event in which the *sancti* participate in these *sancta*.[15]

Notice what Barth has done here. He links the interpretation of the phrase with the comprehensive understanding of the church, the personal view: those sanctified by the Holy Spirit (the *sancti*)—"all Christians of every age and place." This, he has joined with the *sancta*—the communion of holy things. The sanctified, the "holy" participate by their human selves and in their human activities—in "holy things." These "holy things" Barth does not limit to the sacraments, as Abelard did in the medieval church. Instead,

---

14. Calvin, *Institutes* 4.1.3.
15. Barth, *Church Dogmatics*, IV/2, 642-43.

Barth defines the "holy things" as the "holy relationships in which [Christians] stand as *sancti*"[16]—as "holy people." The "holy people" participate in the "holy relationships." These holy relationships are holy gifts, holy tasks to which the holy people are called: the holy positions the people adopt, and the holy functions the people carry out. In all these kinds of activities and relationships the *sancti* (the sanctified, the holy ones) participate: the *sancti* participate in these *sancta*. "The *sancti* are those to whom these *sancta* are entrusted."[17]

Then Barth goes on to enumerate and elaborate what these holy relationships look like in the life of the church. This is his "material definition of the communion of saints." Barth says that "the upbuilding of the community is the communion of saints."[18] The Holy Spirit's work of upbuilding the community—of sanctification—is what is going on in the church. When does the "communion of saints" happen? Barth says it happens in the fellowship of the kinds of activities we participate in as we live and work and serve in the church. See if things he mentions here sound familiar to you.

1. The communion of saints takes place "as the fellowship of Christians in the knowledge and confession of their faith." That is, I would say, as Christians share their faith—beliefs and experiences; and confess their faith in various ways—in words and deeds.

2. The communion of saints takes place, says Barth, "undoubtedly" and "basically" as "a theological and confessional fellowship." We can imagine this means in the theological associations we have in the wider church among other Christians who also confess their faith. We could give a nod to ecumenical activities here, as we live in the one holy catholic church.

3. The communion of saints takes place as the fellowship of "thankfulness and thanksgiving." This is certainly one of the marks of the church, and of our Christian lives: thankfulness and thanksgiving. We are thankful people, grateful people. I wrote a little article for *Presbyterians Today* called "The Rhythm of Our

16. Ibid., IV/2, 643.
17. Ibid.
18. Ibid., 641.

Lives: Grace and Gratitude in the Heidelberg Catechism."[19] Our thankfulness emerges from God's grace in Jesus Christ. In thinking about that article, I turned again to Barth's statement: "Grace evokes gratitude like the voice an echo. Gratitude follows grace like thunder lightning."[20] The hymn we sing at Thanksgiving time is our constant rhythm: "Come, Ye Thankful People, Come." The communion of saints takes place as the fellowship of "thankfulness and thanksgiving."

4. Then in his list, Barth says the communion of saints takes place as "the fellowship of their penitence (leading to conversion), but also with the joy without which there cannot be this penitence in the conversion of the saints." Penitence and joy. Our penitence is for the sin in our lives; our joy is in sin forgiven. This is another rhythm for us. In that article, I quoted the writer Anne Lamott, who said, "Here are the two best prayers I know: 'Help me, help me, help me,' and 'Thank you, thank you, thank you.'"[21] This is the good news of the Christian faith, isn't it: We need help. God helps us in Jesus Christ. We experience joy. The communion of saints is also the community of sinners. But God forgives. In the Christian community, the communion of saints, we experience penitence ... and joy.

5. The communion of saints takes place as "the fellowship of prayer," which, Barth says, "even when it is in the secret chamber, cannot be a private talk with God but only the prayer of the community." Yes, we can—and must—have our "private talk with God." But even as we do, we are aware that we come into God's presence as part of the *communio sanctorum*. We pray to God, prompted by the Holy Spirit, and receiving the intercession of Jesus Christ, as part of the communion of saints, and we also pray *on behalf of* the community of faith. Our prayers go beyond our self-concerns; to the concerns of and for the community—and for the world. Barth had earlier written: "We are either in the *communio sanctorum* or we are not *sancti*. A private monadic faith"—that is, a faith that is

---

19. D. K. McKim, "Rhythm of Our Lives."
20. Barth, *Church Dogmatics*, IV/1, 41.
21. In D. K. McKim, "Rhythm of Our Lives," 49.

The Church

a "monad" (a faith that is self-contained, separate from all else), "a private monadic faith," said Barth, "is not the Christian faith."[22] No monads! Can we think of a better way to get outside ourselves and our little concerns than to pray for the Christian community (other saints) and the world? Our prayers are a context where the communion of saints takes shape.

6. Again, we participate in the communion of the saints, says Barth, "in relationship to the world." This takes place, he says, "as the fellowship of the need of those who are moved by the burdens of the world, and the promise given to it, as their own innermost concern." Are we moved by the "burdens of the world" as well as God's promises—as our "innermost concern"? In the Ecumenical Centre of the World Council of Churches (WCC) in Geneva was held a memorial service for Philip Potter, who died in March 2015 at age ninety-three. Potter was general secretary of the WCC from 1972 to 1984 and was an active, outspoken leader. Potter's wife, Bishop Bärbel Wartenberg-Potter, said at the service that Potter "would often greet the morning by saying, 'Give me my glasses so that we can see what we have to do in the world today.'"[23] Is this the way we greet the morning—putting on our spectacles so we can see what we can be doing in the world today? How are we coming on this? It belongs to the communion of saints to live with this as an "innermost concern."

7. Yet again, the communion of saints takes place as "the fellowship of service in which the saints assist and support one another, and in which they have also actively to attest to those outside what is the will of the One who has taken them apart and sanctified them." The "fellowship of service" is surely something with which we are all familiar. Churches exist to serve, and the community of saints does serve—in countless ways. An important thing is that in the ministries of mutual care and support for one another and in

---

22. Barth, *Church Dogmatics*, IV/1, 678. For more on Barth's view of prayer, see Karl Barth, *Prayer*.

23. World Council of Churches, "Memorial Service Pays Tribute to Philip Potter." http://www.oikoumene.org/en/press-centre/news/memorial-service-pays-tribute-to-philip-potter/.

service to the community we also "actively attest" to the One who has called and is sanctifying us—Jesus Christ, himself. This does not mean we need always to have an active, verbal witness accompanying the forms of support and service we render. But it does mean that we ourselves acknowledge the source and foundation of what we are doing. We are serving others because Jesus Christ has served us. We serve because he serves. As Ernest Campbell said, Christians, like others, may be motivated by the person who says, "*Come* and help." But we are also motivated by the voice of Jesus who says, "*Go* and help."[24] This voice of Jesus is what we are willing to share with others.

8. The communion of saints takes place as "the fellowship of their hope and prophecy looking and reaching beyond the present, but also looking and reaching beyond every temporal future." This is the church in relation to the reign (kingdom) of God. This is the end toward which we move. The church is not the kingdom. But the church looks to, witnesses to, and proclaims the reign of God. This reign of God was the central message of Jesus. Someone asked a little boy what letters follow *A* in the alphabet. And he answered, "All of them." Jesus proclaimed the reign of God; and all else in his life and message followed that.

This reign of God is here in Jesus Christ. When we want to see what the kingdom of God is like, we look to Jesus Christ. As we said above (p. 27), early church theologians said the kingdom was *autobasileia*—a "self-kingdom." The reign of God is embodied in the incarnate Son of God—Jesus Christ. God's reign is here in Christ. But it is still to come. It is the kingdom for which we pray every time we pray in the Lord's Prayer, "Thy kingdom come." Calvin says that "we must every day pray for its coming."[25] I'm sure we do.

9. The communion of saints "above all," said Barth, "takes place as the fellowship of their proclamation of the Gospel, or the Word by which they are gathered and impelled and maintained." Reformed Christians have always accorded preaching of the Word

---

24. Campbell, "What Makes Christian Social Action Different?," 5.
25. Calvin, *Harmony of the Gospels*, 1:208—on Matt 6:10.

a central place. Indeed, Calvin's famous definition of the church is "wherever we see the Word of God purely preached and heard, and the sacraments administered according to Christ's institution."[26] For those who preach regularly, reflect on your preaching preparations... and practices.

Someone described preaching today as "coke and popcorn" preaching. Rather light. You can make your own assessments. That kind of description would not have been welcomed in some earlier times. It would have been an insult, for example, to Dr. George Buttrick, the prominent preacher of the Madison Avenue Presbyterian Church in New York City in the mid-twentieth century. But he had to deal with other comments. He told once of how "a woman came up to him after a worship service and said, 'Dr. Buttrick, since my husband lost his mind, your sermons have come to mean a great deal to him.'"[27]

We hope that Reformed preaching appeals to the mind and heart and moves toward action. Our tradition sees a threefold form of the Word of God. The living Word, Jesus Christ, is made known to us through the written Word, the Scriptures, and made real to us through the Word proclaimed, in preaching. The Word of God gathers, impels, and maintains the communion of saints.

10. Finally, in Barth's top-ten list, he says, "We do not claim this is an exhaustive list." At the end, says Barth, in the context of prayer, the communion of saints happens as "the fellowship of divine service—a liturgical fellowship" that manifests itself as "the fellowship of worship." That is, "the silent and vocal adoration and praise of Almighty God."

In corporate worship we get a glimpse of the local "communion of saints," joined in common "adoration and praise of Almighty God." Through all the varieties of worship styles and practices, this is the constant: "the adoration and praise of Almighty God." Worship is the most important thing we do. How could it not be? To adore and praise our Creator, whose love is

---

26. Calvin, *Institutes* 4.1.9.
27. Wood, "From Past to Future."

given to us in Jesus Christ by the power of the Holy Spirit—what else is worth doing, other than praising?

In worship, said Samuel Miller, over sixty years ago, "We express together what we cannot say alone; we hear together what we cannot hear alone."[28] The Holy Spirit draws the communion of saints together in worship as the community of faith. As Barth put it, "The church service is the most important, momentous and majestic thing which can possibly take place on earth, because its primary content is not [human work: the work of man] but the work of the Holy Spirit and consequently the work of faith."[29] Worship is no casual meeting. Worship engages us fully in "adoration and praise of Almighty God."

Communion of Saints

"I believe in the communion of saints." In one of his books, Alan Walker told the experience of a young minister: "He had been preaching in a tiny village country chapel, and he invited the people to stay for Communion. Only two stayed. He was a little depressed and discouraged at so very small a congregation. So he went on with the ancient ritual a little dully and dejectedly. And then in the course of it he came to the passage: 'With angels and archangels and with all the company of heaven, we worship and adore thy glorious name.' He paused; the wonder gripped him. 'Angels and archangels and all the company of heaven . . .' God forgive me,' he said. 'I did not know I was in that company.'"[30] And yet he was. And so are we.

Summing Up

In brief we have tried to look at some theological dimensions that constitute essentials of ecclesiology. We have seen the church

---

28. Miller, *Life of the Church*, 68.
29. Barth, *Knowledge of God and the Service of God*, 198.
30. Cited in Barclay, *Apostles' Creed for Everyman*, 296–97.

reformed and always being reformed by the Word of God. We have explored our confession: "I believe in the Holy Ghost, the holy catholic church." We have tried to focus on the things most important to say, theologically, about the church—rather than the specific forms the church may take in the years to come.

We live in emerging times. New forms of church are taking shape and will continue to do so. We trust that God is Lord of the church, despite the vicissitudes that come and go. When the church keeps focused on the essentials of ecclesiology, the elements we confess in the Creed, God's Spirit will continue to preserve and keep the church—no matter what forms it takes. The church is a theological community. So theology provides our contexts and our trajectories with Jesus Christ at the center.

In *The Adventures of Tom Sawyer*, Tom Sawyer said to Becky Thatcher, "I been to the circus three or four times—lots of times. Church ain't shucks to a circus." I don't know how the circus is doing these days, but there are people who surely feel like Tom Sawyer: "The church ain't shucks to a circus."

Yet our theological commitment—as disciples of Jesus Christ; as those united by faith with Christ by the work of the Holy Spirit; as the elect of God called to be the people of God, the church, is to be faithful to our calling as Christ's disciples, especially as those called to specific ministries in the church. We can agree with the great Baptist preacher Carlyle Marney when Marney used to say that despite its problems, "the church is still the best thing God's got" to carry out God's work in this world. God uses the likes of us. The church is here in history, "warts and all." Our commitment is to the reform of the church—by the work of God's Word and Spirit. But most of all, our commitment is to Jesus Christ, the Lord of the church. It is he whom we serve. We serve as we confess, I believe in the Holy Ghost, the holy catholic church.

6 Imagine the Church!

In Eph 3:20, we find these words: "Now to him who by the power at work within us is able to accomplish abundantly far more than all we can ask or imagine."

This verse is a doxology or praise to God. It concludes a section in which the writer of Ephesians prays for his readers. He has described the great theological work God has done in the world in sending Jesus Christ, in establishing salvation, in giving the gift of the church as a means by which followers of Christ can live out their Christian lives. He has explained all this and then breaks forth in prayer, asking God to strengthen his readers with power through the Spirit; further he asks that "Christ may dwell in your hearts through faith" so that those in the Ephesian church may "know the love of Christ" and be "filled with all the fullness of God" (3:14–19).

Then, as if he were trying to gather up all those prayers into one, he bursts forth into the doxology. As New Testament scholar Markus Barth translated this verse, the writer is praying "to him who by the power exerted in us is able to outdo superabundantly all that we ask or imagine—Glory to him in the church and in the Messiah Jesus from generation to generation, for ever and ever! Amen."[1] The writer breaks forth, praising the God who has done all those things that have gone before in the Letter to the Ephesians, the God who "by the power exerted in us is able to outdo superabundantly all that we ask or imagine." Imagine that!

---

1. M. Barth, *Ephesians*, 1:367.

The Church

In our Christian faith and in the Reformed and Presbyterian tradition, we have to do with a God who can "outdo superabundantly" all that we can "ask or imagine." This is a fantastic God! This is a God who has done everything we know and believe God has done: everything about which we have read in the Scriptures, everything about which we have heard in the long history of the Christian church, everything we have ever heard our friends and family say God has done in their lives and in the church—this God has done all this, *plus*; *plus* this God can do even more. This God can "outdo superabundantly" all that we can ask . . . or even imagine!

When you come to recognize it is a God like this with whom we are dealing in the Christian faith, what can be more exciting! What can be more thrilling than to be in relationship with a God who will do "far more abundantly" (as older translations say) "than all that we can ask or think"! What can be more exciting than knowing and serving a God who exceeds even our wildest expectations? This is a pure excitement, a pure joy, a pure delight— to live in a relationship of faith, in a God like this! No wonder this doxology has to be sung, in praise! Words alone cannot capture the magnificent vision of what our faith draws us into when we worship and obey and serve this great and glorious God.

Now is this the vision we have of our faith most of the time? Shall we come back down to earth here? Does our Christian faith, and our lives as members of the church provide us with this kind of exciting joy, this kind of huge anticipation for what God is doing in our midst—in the work of the church, in the midst of our own, personal lives? Do we wake each morning, with hearts racing to see what this God, who can do more than we can ever ask or imagine, is up to this day, in our lives?

To be honest, many of us would likely have to confess that this is not the first thought on our minds each morning, or the last thing we think of as we drift off to sleep at night. So much else crowds our days. The busy pragmatics of our lives are usually the main focus of our concerns—paying the bills, picking up the children, managing our jobs. If this God of "superabundant

Imagine the Church!

imagining" is working, this may be hard to see. Our Christian faith is often routine: go to Sunday school, worship, perhaps a committee meeting during the week; then follow the same pattern next week. Where do we find God at work in these amazing ways? Where is the excitement? Where is the joy? It is easy for Christian faith and Christian life to settle into predictable routines—routines that seem natural to us and in which we pass our days and our weeks with not too much thought given to the God whose "power" is being "exerted," or who is "at work" within us.

But three dimensions of our Christian faith, three bumper stickers, if you will, help us recognize and experience this God of superabundance who is at work in the world, in the church, and in our own lives. These bumper stickers are three elements that historically have been important and emphasized by our Reformed and Presbyterian theological traditions. These three elements are parts of our lives as Christians that we will already know about, if we simply stop to think about them. A recovery of the theological resources that have been long been a part of our Presbyterian tradition can help energize our lives as Christians. When we have a stronger theological sense of what is happening in our world, in the church, and in our lives, we will be led to a wider sense, a greater vision, of the God with whom we have to deal and with whom we are related through Jesus Christ in our Christian faith. Theological eyeglasses can improve our perceptions and focus our vision and our imagination to perceive God at work. When we know where to look for the "power exerted in us," we will experience God at work—even in ways beyond "all that we ask or imagine"!

Providence of God

The first theological conviction of our tradition that can enrich our lives and energize our faith is the providence of God.

Providence is a theological doctrine that has been particularly emphasized in our Presbyterian tradition. Most basically, the providence of God emphasizes that the triune God in goodness and power, preserves, accompanies, and directs the universe. Now that's a mouthful, isn't it? But let's unpack it a bit.

The God who created the universe (as we are told in Gen 1:1) has not walked away from the creation. God has not created and then gone fishing! Christians believe the good God who created all things also preserves the creation. God continues to uphold what God has made. What would happen if this were not so? If God created but did not preserve or sustain, the whole creation would collapse. It would collapse away, back into nothingness, because there would be nothing to keep it together. So one aspect of our belief in providence is that God upholds the world.

A second part of providence is that God accompanies or cooperates with the creation. This is especially in regard to us as humans. God upholds and sustains the creation and then enters into relationship and cooperates with us humans, whom God created. God values us and loves us so much that God works *with us* in this world. Think of that! The great, eternal, creating God uses and cooperates with the likes of us—a ragtag group of folks that we are! We are important to God, and God does not treat us as inanimate objects such as stones; instead, God works with us and in us and through us, as human beings. God cooperates with the creation and with us as human beings.

Then a third part of the providence of God is that God directs or governs the universe. This has been a big emphasis for Presbyterians. The providence of God is God's power at work within the world, in and through the natural order, through history, and through people to accomplish God's purposes *in* this world. God is guiding history according to God's will. God is guiding our lives and the life of the church, in accordance with God's will. History has a destination. We call this the kingdom of God or the reign of God. This was the subject that Jesus spoke most about in the Gospels. Jesus spoke more about the kingdom of God than he did about money, sex, or anything else. God's purposes in history are, ultimately, to establish God's reign and God's kingdom in a "new heaven and a new earth." Presbyterians have emphasized that, not only is the eye of God above history, but the hand of God is in history, as Calvin indicated.. God is at work, carrying out divine purposes within our world and within our lives.

Now recognizing this doctrine of the providence of God can enliven and energize our faith. It can comfort us in our faith, and it can challenge us in our faith. We believe, in the words of our Ephesians text, that there is a God whose "power" is being "exerted in us," and that this God is at work in history and in our own lives, and that this God "is able" to "outdo superabundantly all that we ask or imagine." God has a purpose and plan for this world, for the church, and for our own lives. Imagine that!

Imagine this: What if we looked on our routines as church members, not just as a repetition of the same old schedule and processes each week, but what if we looked on them with a lively sense of God's providence being at work? We are being led—in the church and in our lives—to cooperate with God, to accompany God in carrying out God's purposes right here, right now. Isn't that actually tremendously exciting when you think of it? The great, eternal God cuts us in on the action in the world, works within us and among us and through us to carry out God's eternal purposes. Can you think of anything more breathtaking than that? Our days and routines are—if you will, our history is—not just "one darn thing after another." No. Instead, we can look around and believe that God is at work. God is leading us, guiding us, at work in our congregations and in our own lives and ministries—to carry out the purposes that have been (eternally) on God's mind! We are the people God is using in our time and place to accomplish what God wants done in this world. God is at work in our own personal lives, to make us into the persons of faith God wants us to be and to do the things God wants us to do in mission and ministry, as disciples in the church of Jesus Christ!

Having a lively sense of God's providence, God's direction in our lives, and God's presence at work—even in the little things of life—can energize our faith, give us a sense of excitement, and provide a sense of purpose for us that nothing else can give. Just imagine: you are experiencing God's providential purposes, every day. You are cooperating with the great God of "superabundance." Your life is being led and guided by the hand of God in the ways of God's purposes for you. What a comfort this is! And what a challenge. Will we see our lives through theological lenses and recognize the providence of God within and among us? That's our challenge. But our comfort is that we can trust this God who is both great and good, and that God is with us in the midst of all that befalls us. The Puritan theologian William Perkins wrote in the sixteenth century: "When a crosse commeth, it is a hard thing to be patient; but wee must draw our selues thereunto by consideration of God's especiall prouidence."[2] Even when we have to bear a cross, we do so with the faith and trust that the providence of God will see us through. Imagine that: the providence of God!

Presence of Christ

Then comes a second theological conviction. Imagine the presence of Christ.

Our knowledge of God's providence is focused most fully in Jesus Christ. Jesus spoke of God's parental care for us as the children of God quite often. Our faith in Jesus Christ is the lens through which we perceive God's activities among us.

John Calvin defined faith as "knowledge of God's will toward us, perceived from God's Word."[3] Faith "engrafts us in the body of Christ," said Calvin.[4] Faith unites us with Christ so we receive the benefits of all Christ has done. In highly personal terms, Calvin wrote that by faith, "Christ is not outside us but dwells within us. Not only does Jesus Christ cleave to us by an indivisible bond of fellowship, but with a wonderful communion day by day, he grows more and more into one body with us, until he becomes completely one with us."[5] In short, said Calvin, "the whole purpose of the Gospel is that Christ be made ours, and that we be ingrafted

---

2. Perkins, *Exposition of the Symbole*, 1:158.
3. Calvin, *Institutes* 3.2.6.
4. Ibid., 3.2.20.
5. Ibid., 3.2.24.

Imagine the Church!

into His body."[6] So as Christian believers, our "union with Christ" is a very important aspect of Calvin—and later of our own Presbyterian theology.

We are united with Christ, by faith. Faith is the way we perceive the presence of Christ in the church and in our lives. Listen to these words of Calvin which he wrote on Eph 3:17—just three verses before our "imagining" verse (Eph 3:20). Calvin wrote:

> By faith we not only acknowledge that Christ suffered for us and rose from the dead for us, but we receive Him, possessing and enjoying Him as He offers Himself to us. . . . Most consider fellowship with Christ and believing in Christ to be the same thing; but the fellowship which we have with Christ is the effect of faith. The substance of it is that Christ is not to be viewed from afar by faith but to be received by the embrace of our minds, so that He may dwell in us, and so it is that we are filled with the Spirit of God.[7]

Our fellowship with Christ is the "effect of faith"—in both our hearts and our minds. We know that Jesus Christ has died and been raised again to provide the gift of salvation. And now, as Christian people, we are united with Christ, by faith—and live in a relationship with Jesus Christ as our constant companion.

Imagine that! Imagine, living with the full recognition that all our days, all our hours, all our minutes are lived in the presence of Christ, as we are united with Jesus Christ by faith. Doesn't that make Christian life exciting? We live by union with Christ in the bond of faith, which means Jesus Christ is always with us. No situation or circumstance cuts us off from Christ's presence. No difficulty we endure has to be faced alone. When we pray, our prayers do not bounce off the ceiling; they are heard by Jesus, because Christ is always with us. This presence of Christ brings us the "love of Christ" which, as our Ephesians passage says in the

---

6. Calvin, *First Epistle of Paul to the Corinthians*, 24—on 1 Cor 1:9.

7. Calvin, *Epistles of Paul the Apostle to the Galatians, Ephesians, Philippians and Colossians*, 168—on Eph 3:17.

verse before our "imagining" text: "To know the love of Christ that surpasses knowledge" (Eph 3:19).

To realize we receive all the benefits Christ brings in terms of salvation—a new relationship with God, the forgiveness of sin, becoming "new creations"—to realize we receive all this and even more: we receive the presence of Christ himself in us—this is indeed far more than we can "ask or imagine." Is there any greater wonder than this: that God gives us the gift of salvation in Jesus Christ and then unites us by faith with Christ so that we can live constantly in Christ's presence? To see all our days, all our relationships, all our activities as lived out, always, in the presence of Christ can give us a fully alive sense of confidence and joy. We are never alone again; Christ is always with us. We can face all life, no matter what, united with Christ by faith. We have a destiny to dream about as well, because as surely as we live in the presence of Christ here and now, by faith, so surely we will live forever, eternally, with Jesus Christ in the coming kingdom. This can energize our faith. This assures us that we can face life unafraid. This can give us a companion who will never leave us. Imagine that: the presence of Christ!

Power of the Holy Spirit

We live in recognizing the providence of God, the presence of Christ, and then, third, we experience the power of the Holy Spirit. God's power is "at work within us." The power of God's Spirit energizes our church and our lives and launches us into the world in faith to live as the people of God (the church), as Christ's disciples, and as Christians who rely on the Holy Spirit to lead us in the ways of obedience to Christ and in the ways of God's purposes for us.

For Calvin, "the Holy Spirit is the bond by which Christ effectually unites us to himself."[8] Faith is "the principal work of the Holy Spirit."[9] Faith is the "gift of the Spirit." The Holy Spirit

---

8. Calvin, *Institutes* 3.1.1.
9. Ibid., 3.1.4.

illumines us to recognize Scripture as the Word of God.[10] It is the Holy Spirit who gives us the gift of faith—to believe in Jesus Christ as our Lord and Savior.

But the Spirit doesn't stop there. With the gift of faith, we not only believe and trust in Christ, but by the power of the Spirit we are given the gift of being able to look at our lives through the window or lens of faith. That is, by the power of the Spirit, we see the providence of God at work, we see the presence of Christ at work, and we see ways God the Holy Spirit is leading and guiding us in the church and as disciples of Christ into ways of mission and ministry. The Spirit is the energizer of our Christian lives. The Spirit propels us into the world to serve. The Spirit moves among the people of God in the church to help us grow as Christians— through education, through mission, through the love and care of others for us and of us for them. The power of the Spirit can lead us where we have never thought of going ourselves. The Spirit prompts us to prayer, to read the Scriptures, to care for others, to express our faith. The power of the Holy Spirit keeps our lives going, day after day, week after week. The Spirit is active in the routines of our lives—prompting us, nudging us, opening new venues for witness and service. In short, the Spirit enables God in Jesus Christ to "outdo superabundantly all that we ask or imagine"!

Imagine that! God is with us, in Christ, and by the power of the Holy Spirit gives us a brand new world, every day, where we can live out our discipleship and grow in our Christian faith and life. Theologically, we call this process of growth, sanctification. That is, God by the Spirit working within us and among us to enable us to become the Christians (and church members) God wants us to be. Reformed and Presbyterian Christians have always been big on sanctification. We support education in the church—Sunday school, Christian education—so we can grow in our understandings of our Christian faith. We draw people into ministries of service—ministries of care for others, whether it is visiting the sick, or providing food for those in need, or sending folks far away to help those who need the basic necessities of life. We grow in our faith

---

10. Ibid., 3.2.33–34.

The Church

in a variety of ways. But it is the Holy Spirit who opens us to the possibilities and leads and guides as our sanctification continues throughout our lives. We do the routine things, but we do them with excitement because we see that they are not just routines. They are opportunities the Holy Spirit is giving us every day to serve Jesus Christ and carry out the providential purposes of God. Imagine that!

Imagine the Church!

So look at the church and our Christian lives through the theological lenses of our Christian faith and our Presbyterian tradition. When we do, we will find excitement and joy. We can live with a real, vibrant sense of the providence of God, the presence of Christ, and the power of the Holy Spirit. The Trinity supports us; God in three persons leads us into lives where we can sense in both the big things and the little things of life the reality of the God who can "outdo superabundantly all that we ask or imagine"! This is exciting!

William Barclay, the New Testament scholar and writer, told of visiting a church that was very pleasant. It had everything one could imagine for the vestry, the room where the leaders of the worship service put on their robes. But he said, the one thing it lacked was a W.P.B. A W.P.B.—a waste paper basket. Barclay said there are things in life that should be "thrown away," even in the church. And that is what the W.P.B. is for.[11]

But let us take Barclay's insight about the importance of a W.P.B. in a different direction. Most of the time in the church and in our Christian lives, we are rather timid. We say, "Well, if God wants me to do this or that, God will make it plain, God will provide a way, God will let me know what I should do." But instead, what if we think of it the other way around? Try thinking of it in light of recognizing—by faith—the fantastic belief that the providence of God, the presence of Christ, and the power of the Holy

---

11. Barclay, *In the Hands of God*, 83–85.

Imagine the Church!

Spirit is among us! Why not, instead of being timid, be bold? Why not say, "I will launch out in this new venture, this new ministry, this new opportunity"? Why not take the initiative and say that with the providence of God, the presence of Christ, and the power of the Holy Spirit, I will launch out in this new way—and I will *trust* that if God wants to redirect me or reorient me or cause me to cease and desist, God will let me know that? Can we trust God will thus put my plans or purposes into the W.P.B.—the waste paper basket? Why not be bold and launch out in faith, trusting God to do that!

If we lived in our churches and in our Christian lives this way, then just imagine what God could and would do among us and through us and in us! Just imagine! God's power is "exerted in us." God "is able to outdo superabundantly all that we ask or imagine." The excitement of the Christian life in the church is to take steps of radical trust and to see those steps as being led by God, carried out with Jesus Christ at our side, and energized by the power of the Holy Spirit. Look at our lives through these theological lenses and find this excitement!

One more word from John Calvin needs to be said. When Calvin commented on our text, Eph 3:20, he wrote this: "The expression *exceeding abundantly* and *above all that we ask or think*, should be noted, so that there should not be excessive fear in true faith. For however many blessings we expect from God, His infinite liberality will always exceed all our wishes and our thoughts."[12]

Imagine that . . . just imagine that! Calvin wants us to live our faith unafraid. He tells us that "however many blessings we expect from God, His infinite liberality will always exceed all our wishes and our thoughts." Who *knows* what God can do with us if we believe in this great God who loves us in this way! Just imagine the church!

---

12. Calvin, *Epistles of Paul the Apostle to the Galatians, Ephesians, Philippians and Colossians*, 170—on Eph 3:20.

Bibliography

Barclay, William. *In the Hands of God.* New York: Harper & Row, 1966.
———. *The Apostles' Creed for Everyman.* New York: Harper, 1967.
Barth, Karl. *Church Dogmatics.* 4 volumes in 13 parts. Edited by Geoffrey W. Bromiley and T. F. Torrance. Translated by Geoffrey W. Bromiley. Edinburgh: T. & T. Clark, 1956–1967.
———. *The Heidelberg Catechism for Today.* Translated by Shirley C. Guthrie Jr. Richmond: John Knox, 1964.
———. *The Knowledge of God and the Service of God.* Translated by J. L. M. Haire and Ian Henderson. London: Hodder & Stoughton, 1938.
———. *Prayer: 50th Anniversary Edition.* Edited by Don E. Saliers with Essays by I. John Hesselink, Daniel L. Migliore, and Donald K. McKim. Louisville: Westminster John Knox, 2002.
Barth, Markus. *Ephesians.* 2 vols. Anchor Bible 34–34A. Garden City, NY: Doubleday, 1974.
Bavinck, Herman. *Reformed Dogmatics.* Abridged in 1 vol. Edited by John Bolt. Grand Rapids: Baker Academic, 2011.
Benko, Stephen. *The Meaning of Sanctorum Communio.* Studies in Historical Theology 3. Naperville, IL: Allenson, 1964.
Berkouwer, G. C. *The Church.* Translated by James E. Davison. Studies in Dogmatics. Grand Rapids: Eerdmans, 1976.
Bonhoeffer, Dietrich. *The Collected Sermons of Dietrich Bonhoeffer.* Translated by Douglas W. Stott. Edited by Isabel Best. Minneapolis: Fortress, 2012.
———. *Discipleship.* Translated by Barbara Green and Reinhard Krauss. Edited by Geffrey B. Kelly and John D. Godsey. Dietrich Bonhoeffer Works 4. Minneapolis: Fortress, 2001.
Bromiley, Geoffrey W., ed. *Zwingli and Bullinger.* Library of Christian Classics 24. 1953. Reprinted, Louisville: Westminster John Knox, 2006.
Bruner, Frederick Dale, and William E. Hordern. *The Holy Spirit, Shy Member of the Trinity.* Minneapolis: Augsburg, 1984.
Bullock, Robert H., Jr., ed. *Presbyterians Being Reformed: Reflections on What the Church Needs Today.* Louisville: Geneva, 2006.

Bibliography

Calvin, John. *The Acts of the Apostles*: Vol. 1. Edited by David W. Torrance and Thomas F. Torrance. Translated by W. J. G. McDonald. Calvin's New Testament Commentaries. Reprinted, Grand Rapids: Eerdmans, 1979.

———. *The Acts of the Apostles*. Vol. 2. Edited by David W. Torrance and Thomas F. Torrance. Translated by John W. Fraser. Calvin's New Testament Commentaries. Reprinted, Grand Rapids: Eerdmans, 1979.

———. *Calvin: Theological Treatises*. Edited and Translated by J. K. S. Reid. Library of Christian Classics. Philadelphia: Westminster, 1954.

———. *The Epistles of Paul the Apostle to the Galatians, Ephesians, Philippians and Colossians*. Edited by David W. Torrance and Thomas F. Torrance. Translated by T. H. L. Parker. Calvin's New Testament Commentaries. Reprinted, Grand Rapids: Eerdmans, 1980.

———. *The First Epistle of Paul the Apostle to the Corinthians*. Translated by John W. Fraser. Edited by David W. Torrance and Thomas F. Torrance. Calvin's New Testament Commentaries. Reprinted, Grand Rapids: Eerdmans, 1980.

———. *The Gospel according to St. John: Part One 1–10*. Translated by T. H. L. Parker. Edited by David W. Torrance and Thomas F. Torrance. Calvin's New Testament Commentaries. Reprinted, Grand Rapids, Eerdmans, 1979.

———. *The Gospel according to St. John: Part Two 11–21 and The First Epistle of John*. Edited by David W. Torrance and Thomas F. Torrance. Translated by T. H. L. Parker. Calvin's New Testament Commentaries. Reprinted, Grand Rapids: Eerdmans, 1979.

———. *A Harmony of the Gospels Matthew, Mark and Luke Volume 1*. Edited by David W. Torrance and Thomas F. Torrance. Translated by A. W. Morrison. Calvin's New Testament Commentaries. Reprinted, Grand Rapids: Eerdmans, 1980.

———. *Hebrews and 1 and II Peter*. Edited by David W. Torrance and Thomas F. Torrance. Translated by W. B. Johnston, Calvin's New Testament Commentaries. Grand Rapids: Eerdmans, 1973.

———. *Institutes of the Christian Religion*. Edited by John T. McNeill. Translated by Ford Lewis Battles. Library of Christian Classics. Philadelphia: Westminster, 1960.

———. *The Necessity of Reforming the Church*. Translated by Henry Beveridge. London, 1843.

———. *The Second Epistle of Paul to the Corinthians, and the Epistles to Timothy, Titus and Philemon*. Translated by T. A. Smail. Edited by David W. Torrance and Thomas F. Torrance. Calvin's New Testament Commentaries. Reprinted, Grand Rapids: Eerdmans, 1970.

———. *Selected Works of John Calvin*. Edited by Henry Beveridge and Jules Bonnet. 7 vols. Reprinted, Grand Rapids: Baker, 1983.

Campbell, Ernest T. "Follow Me." A sermon preached in the Riverside Church in the City of New York. Riverside Sermons. February 27, 1970. http://www.archive.org/stream/sermonfollowmeoocamp#page/no/mode/2up.

Bibliography

———. "The Christian Way of Seeing." A sermon preached in the Riverside Church in the City of New York. Riverside Sermons. May 25, 1969. https://archive.org/details/sermonchristianwoocamp.

———. "What Makes Christian Social Action Different?" A sermon preached in the Riverside Church in the City of New York. Riverside Sermons. May 24, 1970. Available at http://www.archive.org/stream/sermonwhatmakescoocamp#page/no/mode/2up.

Campi, Emidio. *Shifting Patterns of Reformed Tradition*. Reformed Historical Theology 27. Göttingen: Vandenhoeck & Ruprecht, 2014.

Copeland, A. J. "Why Lead?" *Christian Century* 130/23 (Nov. 13, 2013), 11–12.

Dulles, Avery. *The Catholicity of the Church*. Oxford: Clarendon, 1985.

Fison, J. E. *The Blessing of the Holy Spirit*. Libra Books. New York: Longmans, Green, 1950.

Jay, Eric G. *The Church: Its Changing Image through Twenty Centuries*. Atlanta: John Knox, 1980.

Kärkkäinen, Veli-Matti, ed. *Holy Spirit and Salvation*. Sources of Christian Theology. Louisville: Westminster John Knox, 2010.

Kelly, J. N. D. *Early Christian Creeds*. 3rd ed. London: Longman, 1972.

Küng, Hans. *The Church*. Translated by Ray and Rosalee Ockenden. New York: Sheed & Ward, 1967.

Levering, Matthew. *Engaging the Doctrine of the Holy Spirit: Love and Gift in the Trinity and the Church*. Grand Rapids: Baker Academic, 2016.

Manson, T. W. *Ethics and the Gospel*. London: SCM, 1960.

McKee, Elsie Anne. *The Pastoral Ministry and Worship in Calvin's Geneva*. Travaux d'humanisme et Renaissance 556. Geneva: Droz, 2016.

McKim, Donald K. *Introducing the Reformed Faith: Biblical Revelation, Christian Tradition, Contemporary Significance*. Louisville: Westminster John Knox, 2001.

———, ed. *Readings in Calvin's Theology*. 1984. Reprinted, Eugene, OR: Wipf & Stock, 1998.

———. *Theological Turning Points: Major Issues in Christian Thought* Atlanta: John Knox, 1988.

———. "The Rhythm of Our Lives: Grace and Gratitude in the Heidelberg Catechism." *Presbyterians Today* (May 2015) 48–49.

McKim, LindaJo H., ed. *The Presbyterian Hymnal*. Louisville: Westminster John Knox, 1990.

McNeill, John T. *Unitive Protestantism: The Ecumenical Spirit and Its Persistent Expression*. Richmond, VA: John Knox, 1964.

Merriam-Webster's Collegiate Dictionary. 11th ed. Springfield, MA: Miriam-Webster, 2003.

Miller, Samuel. *The Life of the Church*. New York: Harper, 1953.

Minear, Paul. *Images of the Church in the New Testament*. 1960. Reprinted, New Testament Library. Louisville: Westminster John Knox, 2004.

Moltmann, Jürgen. *The Church in the Power of the Spirit*. Translated by Margaret Kohl. New York: Harper & Row, 1977.

Bibliography

———. "*Theologia Reformata et Semper Reformanda.*" In *Toward the Future of Reformed Theology: Tasks, Topics, Traditions*, edited by David Willis and Michael Welker, 120–35. Grand Rapids: Eerdmans, 1999.

Perkins, William. *The Workes of the Famous and Worthy Minister of Christ in the Universitie of Cambridge, Mr. William Perkins*. 3 vols. London: Legatt, 1616–1618.

Presbyterian Church (U.S.A.). *Book of Confessions: Study Edition*. Louisville: Geneva, 1999. Office of the General Assembly, 2016.

———. *The Constitution of the Presbyterian Church (U.S.A.). Part I, Book of Confessions*. Louisville: Office of the General Assembly 2016.

———. *The Constitution of the Presbyterian Church (U.S.A.). Part II, Book of Order 2015–2017*. Louisville: Office of the General Assembly, 2015.

Purdy, John C., ed. *Always Being Reformed: The Future of Church Education*. Philadelphia: Geneva, 1985.

Robbins, Anna M., ed. *Ecumenical and Eclectic: The Unity of the Church in the Contemporary World*. Studies in Christian History and Thought. Milton, Keynes, UK: Paternoster, 2007.

Rogers, Jack B., and Donald K. McKim, *The Authority and Interpretation of the Bible: An Historical Approach*. 1979. Reprinted with a new epilogue, Eugene, OR: Wipf & Stock, 1999.

Schultz, Charles M. *The Complete Peanuts*, Vol. 5, *1959–1960*. Seattle: Fantagraphics, 2015.

Selderhuis, Herman J., ed. *Calvinus sacrarum literarum interpres*. Papers of the International Congress on Calvin Research. Reformed Historical Theology 5. Göttingen: Vandenhoeck & Ruprecht, 2008.

Thiselton, Anthony C. *The Holy Spirit—in Biblical Teaching, through the Centuries, and Today*. Grand Rapids: Eerdmans, 2013.

Thompson, John. *The Holy Spirit in the Theology of Karl Barth*. Princeton Theological Monographs Series 23. Allison Park, PA: Pickwick Publications, 1991.

Wandel, Lee Palmer. *Reading Catechisms, Teaching Religion*. Brill Studies in Intellectual History 250. Brill's Studies on Art, Art History, and Intellectual History 11. Leiden: Brill, 2016.

Warfield, Benjamin Breckenridge. *Calvin and Augustine*. Edited by Samuel G. Craig. Reprinted, Philadelphia: Presbyterian & Reformed, 1974.

Welker, Michael. *God the Spirit*. Translated by John F. Hoffmeyer. Minneapolis: Fortress, 1994.

———. "The Holy Spirit." *Theology Today* 46 (1989) 5–20.

Willis, David, and Michael Welker, eds. *Toward the Future of Reformed Theology: Tasks, Topics, Traditions*. Grand Rapids: Eerdmans, 1999.

Williams, Rowan. *On Christian Theology*. Challenges in Contemporary Theology. Oxford: Blackwell, 2001.

Wood, William P. "From Past to Future." Sermon preached on May 30, 2010, at First Presbyterian Church in Charlotte, North Carolina. http://www.firstpres-charlotte.org/sermons/20100530-1100.pdf/.

World Council of Churches. "Memorial Service Pays Tribute to Philip Potter." May 18, 2015. http://www.oikoumene.org/en/press-centre/news/memorial-service-pays-tribute-to-philip-potter/.

Made in the USA
Columbia, SC
16 October 2018